W9-AAI-695

JUST ONE THING

JUST ONE THING

Twelve of the World's Best Investors Reveal the One Strategy You Can't Overlook

JOHN MAULDIN, Editor

WILEY

JOHN WILEY & SONS, INC.

Published by John Wiley & Sons, Inc., Hoboken, New Jersey.
Published simultaneously in Canada.

For general information on our other products and services or for technical support, please contact our Customer Care Department within the United States at (800) 762-2974, outside the United States at (317) 572-3993, or fax at (317) 572-4002.

Wiley also publishes its books in a variety of electronic formats. Some content that appears in print may not be available in electronic books. For more information about Wiley products, visit our Web site at www.wiley.com.

Library of Congress Cataloging-in-Publication Data:

Mauldin, John.
    Just one thing : twelve of the world's best investors reveal the one
  strategy you can't overlook / John Mauldin.
        p.   cm.
    Includes bibliographical references.
    ISBN-13: 978-0-471-73873-2 (cloth)
    ISBN-10: 0-471-73873-5 (cloth)
    1. Investments—Handbooks, manuals, etc.   I. Title: Twelve of the world's
  best investors reveal the one strategy you can't overlook.   II. Title.
    HG4527.M365 2006
    332.67'8—dc22
                                                    2005025979

Printed in the United States of America.
10 9 8 7 6 5 4 3 2 1

CONTENTS

INTRODUCTION

"Just One Thing," I told them.

"Give me the one best investing concept that you want to pass on to your kids."

One of the great things about working in my field is that I get to run around with some very smart people. I get to pick their brains and learn from the best. If you could get a chance to sit down with a Gartman or Kessler or any of the other contributors to this book you would undoubtedly leap at the chance. What one thing could each of them tell you that would make a difference in your investing life? It's impossible to calculate the value of one idea if it helps us become better investors, or saves us the pain of losses.

I asked the contributors to share their insights. The authors of these chapters have all learned a lot along the way. "Why not," I thought, "ask them to share the wealth of their wisdom?" And so I did. There were no rules, so that's why the chapters vary in length and topic.

What I wanted to get was material that would be readable and accessible to the average investor. Nothing is more frustrating to me than a great idea I can't understand. I asked them to make it something that will give readers an "aha" moment. Just share it with us.

Now, I could guess what a few of them would write about before I asked. Mark Finn was going to write about the problems of past performance. He is absolutely brilliant on that (and a lot of other things), which is why he gets big institutions to keep coming back for his consulting. And you knew that Dennis Gartman would write on his Rules of Trading. Gartman has forgotten more about trading than most of us will ever know. Which, he would tell you, is why he writes his rules down so he can remember them and follow them! You break these rules, you are gonna lose. If you want to trade, you need these near your desk.

But I didn't know how some of the other contributors could

narrow their advice down to Just One Thing. That was hard. But they have all done a great job.

Okay, Andy Kessler gives us two. But when you turn $100 million into a cool $1 billion and get out at the top, two ideas are a good thing. Kessler shows how investing in what everyone knows is how to get just average returns (or less!). Better, he says, to invest like you are walking in a fog.

Gary Shilling shows us the value of one really good idea. George Gilder tells us that in fact inside information is the best information. Want to average almost 3 percent a year better on your funds? Rob Arnott writes compellingly that the way index (and many mutual) funds are currently constructed is inefficient, and he offers a new way to invest. This powerful analysis could be worth a lot to you.

Bill Bonner first tells us that we need to start with a principle if we want to succeed and then shows us his idea as to what that is. Mike Masterson looks at the same thought, but comes away with an entirely different take.

James Montier gives us a very thorough overview of the latest research on the human foibles in investing. He is an expert on the psychology of investing, having literally written the book on the subject. This chapter is one you will want to read and reread and come back to often.

Richard Russell, who has been writing since 1958 and is the dean of economics writers, gives us his thoughts on time, hope, and the power of compounding. Anytime Richard talks, we should listen. Ed Easterling shows us that "risk is not a knob to be turned for greater returns." "The first step toward making money is not losing it," he writes, and shows us how to avoid unnecessary risk while making it our friend when we do encounter it.

And finally, I weigh in with a few thoughts on the power of change in our future. The pace of change is accelerating, and we need to know not only what is changing but how to take advantage of it. The best investments of the next 20 years will be those that are a part of the process of change.

I am proud of this book and the work my friends have done to bring you their one best idea. I believe you will find many nuggets you can use in your own life and investing. As to the order of the chapters, it was just too much to decide who should be first and then second and so on; each chapter deserves to be a lead chapter. So I let the way they were organized in my inbox be the prime factor. You can start at the beginning or in the middle or the end, but read them all.

And Just One More Thing: There are a lot of great ideas in the next few hundred pages, but you have to put them into practice. So as you read, think about how you will put the principles, tips, and ideas to use in your personal life. And that will make this book be a very good thing.

CHAPTER 1

Signposts in the Fog

∽

Andy Kessler is a modern-day Investment Renaissance Man. He does it all. He was a research analyst and investment banker for some of the biggest firms on Wall Street. He wrote about his experiences in his first book, Wall Street Meat. *He then went on to co-found Velocity Capital Management, a hedge fund that raised $80 million. Kessler turned it into a cool $1 billion in a matter of five years, and then got out at the top! He chronicled those days in the book* Running Money. *He now writes* Wall Street Journal *op-eds, as well as articles for* Forbes *and* Wired, *and appears frequently on CNBC, CNN, Fox News, and Dateline NBC. And he stays in top physical shape by keeping up with his four sons!*

His latest book, How We Got Here, *talks about industrial development, from the steam engine through the Internet. Andy lives in Northern California with his wife and four sons and is working on a mysterious new project, which he promises to share with me once he has it figured out. You can find out more about Andy at www.andykessler.com, where you can also get a free download of his latest book.* —John Mauldin

∽

Signposts in the Fog

by Andy Kessler

∽

YEARS AGO, I DECIDED TO CLIMB MOUNT WASHINGTON, DRAGGING A RELUC-
tant friend, Paul, along with me. It was a beautiful August morning
in New Hampshire, not a cloud in the sky, birds chirping—couldn't
be better. Paul ran marathons and had already run eight miles that
morning but agreed to my "little hike." He still had his running
clothes on; I was sporting a fresh Blue Öyster Cult T-shirt.

We parked the car and found the trailhead. Next to the usual
warnings about poison ivy and rabid squirrels hung a huge sign
that read, "STOP. The area ahead has the worst weather in America.
Many have died there from exposure, even in the summer. Turn
back now if the weather is bad."

I looked up at the cloudless sky and said sarcastically, "Looks
pretty bad to me; let's roll."

The climb was strenuous, for me anyway, but not a killer. At
some point the trees gave way to rocks, the temperature dropped,
and a fog bank came out of nowhere to sit not 10 feet above our
heads. We kept climbing until we were engulfed in the fog.

"Any idea where the trail is, Einstein?" Paul asked.

"No."

"I can't see a damn thing."

"I heard there were trail markers—signposts or something," I
said.

"Like that?" Paul asked, pointing to a barely visible yellow rock
sitting on top of a vertical stack of four larger rocks.

We headed through the fog to the yellow rock. When we got
there, we were almost able to make out another yellow rock on another stack 10 or 15 feet away. And so we proceeded, making out
signposts in the fog, slowly, surely—steady progress, freezing our

3

asses off. At one point we couldn't make out anything. You could barely see your feet. I wasn't sure if I was making out yellow rocks or just hallucinating; but we kept heading upward and, sure enough, found another yellow rock, closer to our goal.

It stopped being fun, but it was sure exhilarating. Around two in the afternoon, hungry, cold, and barely speaking, we made it to the top of Mount Washington. Rather than planting a flag, we headed into the restaurant and fought the crowds who took the Cog Railway, drove, or were bussed to the top. Paul and I both bought rather overpriced Mount Washington sweatshirts, wolfed down greasy cheeseburgers, and hung out for about five minutes until Paul said, "Ready to head down the hill?" This time we knew what we were doing.

And that, my friends, is how I learned how to invest.

INVESTING IN THE FOG

Investing is hard—as hard as Chinese arithmetic, as another friend of mine used to say. It's onerous, treacherous, humiliating, and subject to extreme weather conditions.

My old partner Fred Kittler said it best: "The stock market trades to inflict the maximum amount of pain." I don't know about you, but I have a very low threshold of pain. Yet I spent a career on Wall Street, first as an analyst following volatile technology companies, as an investment banker, a venture capitalist, and finally running what ended up as a billion-dollar hedge fund.

I did it by investing in the fog.

YOU CAN'T MAKE MONEY STANDING IN THE SUNSHINE

As any junior-year "Stocks for Jocks" course will tell you, a stock price is nothing more than the net present value of a company's future earnings. How easy is that? All you need to know is how much a company is earning today, how fast it is growing, and what discount rate to apply to future earnings to get that net present value.

This reminds me of the *Saturday Night Live* routine with Chevy Chase playing President Gerald Ford in the election debates. Asked about the effect of inflation on budget deficits, Ford/Chase answers, "Uh, I was told there wouldn't be any math."

On any given day, the math is quite easy. Widgets 'R' Us earned a dollar per share last year. Its growth rate was 12 percent. The inflation deflator is 2.83 percent; hence, the stock is worth exactly $18.42. You can get the formula out of any good economics textbook. Good luck with that.

Maybe the stock really is $18.42. Maybe it's $20 and you should short it, or maybe it's $15 and you should buy it. I wouldn't touch it either way. Why?

Because everybody already knows about the $1, 12 percent, 2.83 percent deflator. The sun is shining bright. Say what you want about the efficient market theory, if everybody knows something, you ain't gonna make money on it. "But the widget business is growing nicely," you tell me. Yeah, so what? We don't live in a static world. As my baby's bib reads, "Spit happens."

The widget business is not going to stay that way. It's either going to get better or it's going to get worse; but unless they are cooking the books, it's not going to grow exactly 12 percent for the foreseeable future. Yet the stock, today at least, is valued for 12 percent growth.

Inputs to the model change every day. That's why the stock market is open Monday through Friday. That's why it is never closed more than one day a week during holidays. Values of companies change. There are a lot of inputs to those silly formulas, almost none of them written in concrete. Sales need to be closed. Profits need to be earned. Spending plans at the beginning of a quarter only guess at how much revenue might support them. Growth is based on global economics. A butterfly batting its wings in Indonesia won't necessarily change stock values, but a coup in Thailand just might (such events happen every couple of years).

Formulas rarely have an input for risk. Even if they did, it's an unquantifiable number. A risk-adjusted growth rate is about as specific as economists can come up with.

The problem with Widgets 'R' Us, the stock anyway, is that it's out in the open, right out there in the sunshine. Everybody can see it. Everybody agrees on its prospects. Whoop-dee-doo. The weather's gonna change.

I'd rather be out in the fog where nobody knows nothin'. Then, if I'm good, I can peer out into the fog and spot some yellow rocks to show the way to a higher level. Once I get to the signpost, it's quite clear, and my stocks based on getting to that signpost will be properly valued; so I slog on looking for the next signpost.

THE IMPORTANCE OF SPOTTING
THE SIGNPOSTS IN THE FOG

If I haven't scared you away from investing yet, you are either persistent or a fool. That's good; one of these is a good attribute for successful investing.

This whole idea of investing in the fog is *not* about being a contrarian. It's about seeing things before others. If you think everybody is going to sit in Starbucks sipping lattes using laptops connected to the Internet via Wi-Fi (like I am now), that's a pretty investable idea. There might be half a dozen interesting investment ideas that would benefit from that trend. But might I suggest that you look around Starbucks, and if everyone is already sitting around sipping and surfing, you are too late. The stock market already knows about it and has discounted the potential growth for chip software and service companies. Sip enough lattes, and you too can hallucinate the future.

Investing in the fog is about seeing things others can't. Most people get in the fog and panic; but the trick is to get in the fog and feel comfortable, let your imagination run wild, imagine what things might look like up ahead, make out vague outlines in the distance, and invest as if those outlines were real things.

I remember a comedian on *Ed Sullivan* (I'm dating myself, I know, but it was funny) saying his mother-in-law drank so much, she saw color television years before anyone else. Get her a fund to run!

Over time, if those outlines become real, or even close to being real, you will have invested at such a discount to the eventual value that you will make a killing. Just don't forget that you are no longer in the fog when you can see what was once an outline and is now living breathing reality. Get ye back into the fog. The stock market always looks ahead. A great investor has a continued paranoia concerning who knows what, what they know, and when they knew it.

Step onto any trading desk or into any money management firm and you enter a bizarre world. Lots of screens, all filled with blinking information. Stock prices, headlines, press releases, news stories, CNBC on monitors scattered around the room, often muted. Money managers read the *Wall Street Journal* cover to cover, the *New York Times* business section, *Barron's* on weekends, scan *Forbes* and *Fortune*, have their assistants read *BusinessWeek*, subscribe to thestreet.com, get MarketWatch e-mail alerts, and scan message boards on Yahoo! and Motley Fool. And that's before the market opens. They also get e-mails from every major brokerage firm, with comments from their Morning Calls, what analysts have to say about everything. Bigger firms get calls from salesmen and saleswomen from Wall Street with a synopsis, and then the analysts call as the day goes on to provide color. Every firm I know has expanded its voicemail systems, which would often stop accepting messages by 10 a.m., so full of hyperbabble they were.

Do they get stock ideas from all this stuff? I highly doubt it. The fire hose of information is for one reason and one reason only—to take the pulse of the market and figure out what everyone else already knows. Information is sunshine. I want to know everything, because then and only then can I know if my investment ideas are already out there—or are they still just figments of my twisted mind, outlines in the fog, flutters in my gut.

The trick is to figure out what the fire hose of information overload is going to say in three months, six months, 18 months, even three to five years if you are really patient. When all that information is blaring loud and clear what you squinted to see way back when, then that's it, it's over, you win. The market has caught up with you and is sitting right on top of the yellow rock you could barely make out before. You get the return for seeing it first when no one else believed it. The stocks you own based on that trend are now worth not 20 percent or 30 percent more, but two times, three times, ten times more. Now that's investing.

PICKING THE RIGHT SIGNPOSTS

Okay, okay, enough about fog and sunshine, I think you get the point. So what are these signposts or trail markers I'm talking about? Quite simply, they are big trends that you believe in, have confidence in, know in your gut to be true, have 99.99 percent probability of coming to fruition. These aren't picked randomly or without lots of work, tons of sweat, and consternation. As my hero Bullwinkle once said, holding up a drawing of two people, "This is Froth with Portent."

Pick the wrong trend and you are following signposts off a cliff. Sometimes worse—pick too obvious a trend and you'll never find your way *into* the fog to discover the hidden paths to riches. In the twenty years I spent on Wall Street, I have only been able to find two real signposts for investing in the fog. Two. How lame, really. I was a professional, recommending stocks and then running a billion of other people's money, and it was all based on two stinking trends.

Yup. But what wonderful trends they were—probably still are.

I thought about writing ten or fifteen more paragraphs about how cool these trends are and then suggest you send a thousand dollars in small bills to a post office box in Palo Alto and then I might tell you one of them. But what the heck, I've written a couple of books that more or less spilled the beans, so here they are (drum roll please):

- Elasticity: lower cost creates its own huge markets.
- Intelligence moves out to the edge of the network.

If you're disappointed and saying, "Huh? That's it? You made me read this stupid chapter and that's all I get?" take it easy and let me explain.

Elasticity in the Marketplace

Back in 1985 and 1986, I was a 26-year-old know-nothing-about-stocks electrical engineer hired to be the semiconductor analyst at PaineWebber in New York. The industry had just seen a jolt of orders in 1985 and then a big whopping recession by April of 1986. Intel, TI,

Motorola, and AMD all saw their stocks plummet. Orders dried up and prices for memory and microprocessors were plummeting.

I somehow figured out it was distributors buying chips in 1985, not IBM, so I actually had one of the rare sell recommendations on these stocks. My star was rising on Wall Street. With these stocks headed to hat sizes 6-7/8, 7 . . . I was looking for an excuse to turn around and recommend them. I read an article in *Electronics* magazine about EPROMs—Eraseable Programmable Read-Only Memories. It suggested that every time prices dropped for EPROMs, some new device would use them, or use more EPROM—16,000 bits instead of 1,000 bits (remember, this was 1986!).

Videogames, PCs, modems, each of them would somehow design in more EPROMs, or denser EPROMs, whenever prices collapsed; and at some point, when the cycle turned, even though prices were still low, sales would increase because more EPROMs would be sold. I looked it up, and the word that describes this phenomenon is *elasticity*.

As an engineer, I was forced to take Econ 101 (and blew away econ majors because they couldn't handle the math), but not much else on the econ or financial front. Good thing. Elasticity is one of those things that doesn't model well. Economists don't understand it, so they don't talk about it much (except for things that are inelastic, like cigarettes and booze, which economists may have a bit too much of).

So anyway, I went to work on this wacky concept of elasticity of chips and semiconductors, looked back in time at other cycles, and sure enough, it was real. Intel founder Gordon Moore made the observation that chip density doubles every eighteen months (in *Electronics* magazine, it turns out), and Moore's Law was relentless. Elasticity is just the financial explanation of how the industry grows whenever prices of bits or gates or functions drop. The industry magically grows (and stocks eventually go up), and a smart semiconductor analyst would get ahead of this curve.

So I went out with that call. Done selling? Great, now buy back Intel and Motorola, because elasticity will kick in and this will be a great growth market for microprocessors with faster and faster clock speeds.

I got a lot of "what the hell are you talking about" looks from my portfolio manager clients. Oddly, I was used to this look from friends and family.

So I calmly explained that every time prices dropped, some new application would open up to take advantage of the cheaper functionality. Told them I wouldn't be surprised if we saw laser printers put all that cheap memory into them to print pages faster and cheaper. Lucky for me, desktop publishing was soon born, and my elasticity argument proved out.

I've been milking this old elasticity thing ever since.

In 1996 my partner and I started Velocity Capital with the simple premise that while semiconductor elasticity was still playing out (and still, no one on the Street really understood it), telecommunications bandwidth would follow the same pattern. As bandwidth to businesses and homes got cheaper, new applications would open up to take advantage of the cheaper functionality. Modem speeds went from 14.4K to 56K to 256K DSL to 1 meg cable modem. Ten-megabit-per-second local area networks moved to 100 megabit to gigabit. Fiber optics brought multi-gigabit speeds. The Internet and all its permutated businesses were the new applications.

In practice, with every company we looked at, my partner would assess management (I never trusted anyone), and then the two of us would think out elasticity for the company. We would try to map out the next two to five years of products or services. If we couldn't figure out how the company could scale and benefit from elasticity, we would not walk, but run away as fast as we could.

Talk about the fog: In 1996 most people would respond "how cute" to our idea of bandwidth elasticity. By 1999 it was every investor's mantra in some form or another.

Elasticity still works. Bandwidth prices are in the gutter, but I'll bet end demand is still elastic. More memory goes into cameras and phones, faster microprocessors go into PCs, 10-gigabit networks are rolling out, and on and on.

Still investable? Perhaps.

But I'll bet you can find your own elastic markets (e-mail them to me and I'll send the best five ideas a Blue Öyster Cult T-shirt).

Does the healthcare business scale? Not obviously, but some

part of it must. Aspirin is a drug that was elastic over the years. Most prescription drugs are inelastic, but something might break out.

Financial services can exhibit elasticity—talk to Charles Schwab. Autos? Electronics content is rising. And on and on. Look deep, find the elasticity, and you'll be in the middle of the fog with signposts to lead the way.

Finding Intelligence at the Outer Edges

I know this book is titled *Just One Thing*, and I'm about to describe a second trend, but really, it's just a byproduct of elasticity. It's what happens when you have all these cheap PCs and smartphones and ever-cheaper bandwidth scattered around.

Sometimes you are not able to recognize elasticity, or maybe everybody already does recognize it—but if it jumps out at you, so much the better.

A sage person once noted:

> The network is too large to have all its affairs directed by a single central entity. Control at such a distance, and from under the eye of their constituents, must be unable to administer and overlook all the details necessary for the good governance of the users; and the same circumstance, by rendering detection impossible to their users, will invite agents to corruption, plunder and waste.

Who said this? Bill Gates? Bernie Ebbers? Michael Powell? Actually, it was Thomas Jefferson in 1800 (okay, I swapped *country* for *network* and *government* for *entity*, but the concept is there). Jefferson's federalist beliefs were driven by his agrarian upbringing and fear of centralized control, but actually he would have made a great tech geek.

There is a saying out here in Silicon Valley that most people live and invest by: *"Intelligence moves out to the edge of the network."* It explains the proliferation of PCs, iPods, smartphones, Tivos, GPS maps, digital cameras, and every other gadget on the constantly declining cost treadmill in techland. This is a world of few regulations, nine-month product cycles, and a mix of massive wealth and broken dreams.

For those who live east of the Sierra Nevadas, you most likely feel the heavy hand of Hamiltonian central planners stamping out innovation. Almost every network invented before 1983 is controlled by old analog monopolies—SBC, Comcast, Cingular, Time-Warner Cable, Verizon. Rules are set by government committees. Prices are set by collusion—er, lobbied regulators. Innovation is limited to call waiting and news crawls. The center of the network is sclerotic and milked for the benefit of moguls first and shareholders second. Users are a distant last. These guys love to be regulated, as it freezes technology and innovation and business models in their tracks.

Ask SBC. It charges $20 a month for a phone service that should cost pennies. It has drab phones with twelve buttons at the edge and expensive switches and zillions of lines of code running at control centers in the network. Meanwhile, you can download a program called Skype to talk from PC to PC for free. Same service, voice in, voice out. Twenty bucks versus free. What gives?

It's the network, stupid. Literally. The beauty of the Internet is that it is plain old stupid—Blaster, not Master. Packets of information fly around effortlessly. They contain an address where they are a-comin' from and where they are a-goin'. Cisco and Juniper are two companies that make routers that move trillions of these packets around, like an octopus on speed. What is in the packet is of no concern—a Web page, a Google search result, Amazon book order, voice call to Vanuatu, pirated videos of *Dodgeball*—it doesn't matter. The network is a sprinter, not a quarterback.

Why should you care? As the post-Internet-boom phone companies consolidate, cheerleaders of these deals see a return of giants who can afford the massive spending to bring fiber to every home and business in America. Will we get it? Yup, but not from them.

The day of the Verizon–MCI deal announcement, CNBC's Dylan Ratigan interviewed Verizon CEO Ivan Seidenberg and MCI CEO

Michael Cappellas. Neither could articulate why they wanted to do this deal, until this doozy came out of Ivan's mouth:

> We need to install networks, because networks represent our lifeblood to the customer. All the intelligence gets put into the network—all the interesting features and function get put into the network.

This is what Jefferson was warning us about. Forget gadgets, Verizon wants to offer all the services it thinks you need in the network. Its track record is lame. It took Bell Labs several years to develop and certify call waiting; three-way calling took a bit longer. Caller ID took a decade and still doesn't really work.

Meanwhile, a clever programmer chugging Jolt cola can pull an all-nighter (with a few breaks for Nerf gun battles) and add features to Internet calling. Want eight-way calling? No problem. CD-quality voice? Simple. Transcripts from your last three conversations? Done.

When intelligence is out at the edge of the network, making changes or ramping innovation is simple. I know it sounds bizarre, but as long as the connecting network is dumb, the value of the network can increase.

Cellular companies have barely added features to their basic service, so they keep inventing calling plans to confuse us into paying more. But meanwhile, by opening a browser on my phone and moving packets through a dumb Internet versus "smart" voice network, I can pull up maps and directions.

Thank you, Thomas Jefferson.

The best example of intelligence at the edge is one that may not be so obvious: Google.

A hundred thousand servers sitting in data centers programmed by 2,000 programmers with doctorates doesn't sound like intelligence at the edge, but it really is. Minitel in France was a breakthrough twenty years ago by providing pages of information for the French. Weather, news, train schedules. It was centrally managed. Any new pages had to be programmed by the folks at Minitel, at much time and expense. Google, by contrast, doesn't tell you what you are searching for; it scours the edge of the network for that information and uses an algorithm to calculate if it might be what you are looking for. The smart servers hosting Web pages and the millions of users with PCs putting up those Web pages are the intelligence at the edge. There are billions of Web pages to crawl, specifically because the intelligence is at the edge versus the center.

Subtle stuff perhaps, but I can sniff out a short-lived business, even if it is regulated to exist, if it violates this principle.

The good news is that our networks are getting dumber and our devices at the edge are getting smarter and better everyday. Megapixel cameras, programmable TVs, GPS-enabled phones—the possibilities are endless, at the edge.

A GLANCE BACK AT SATISFACTION AND REWARDS

After climbing Mount Washington, Paul and I got back to our car, hot from wearing Mt. Washington sweatshirts in such nice, cloudless weather on a summer day in New Hampshire. At the bottom of that hill we just climbed, anyway. And we were famished, in that "I could eat a horse" mood.

I got out a map, found the road that led due east, broke several state and federal speed-limit laws, and hit the coast of Maine a couple of hours later.

We pulled into the first shack we could find and ordered three 1-pound lobsters each—a just reward for the day and a perfect metaphor to reflect back upon.

CHAPTER 2

The "Not-So-Simple" (But Really Utterly So) Rules of Trading

∽

Dennis Gartman is the trader's trader. He is up at 2 to 3 a.m. and writes a daily letter (the eponymous The Gartman Letter*) every morning by 6 a.m. Eastern time, wherever he is in the world. He analyzes the currency, commodity, energy, and metals markets, and has been doing so for nearly twenty years. A wide range of people read Gartman—the rich and famous, the small investor along with staffers at nearly every major trading house and fund in the world. His wisdom and insights are often seen on TV, and he is in constant demand as a speaker at investment conferences. He has forgotten more about trading than most people will ever know. He trades every day, and his trades are on the record for all the world to see.*

Dennis is one of my best sources for ideas and is a great sounding board. He lives in Suffolk, Virginia, and is a five handicap golfer. His one "vice" (that I know of) is a penchant for great hotels and big suites when he travels—which is a lot, so he deserves it. —John Mauldin

∽

The "Not-So-Simple" (But Really Utterly So) Rules of Trading

by Dennis Gartman

∽

THE WORLD OF INVESTING/TRADING, EVEN AT THE VERY HIGHEST LEVELS, where we are supposed to believe that wisdom prevails and profits abound, is littered with the wreckage of wealth that has hit the various myriad rocks that exist just beneath the tranquil surface of the global economy. It matters not what level of supposed wisdom, or education, that the money managers or individuals in question have. We can make a list of wondrously large financial failures that have come to flounder upon these rocks for the very same reasons. Let us, for a bit, have a moment of collective silence for Long Term Capital Management; for Barings Brothers; for Sumitomo Copper . . . and for the tens of thousands of individuals each year who follow their lead into financial oblivion.

I've been in the business of trading since the early 1970s as a bank trader, as a member of the Chicago Board of Trade, as a private investor, and as the writer of *The Gartman Letter*, a daily newsletter I've been producing for primarily institutional clientele since the middle 1980s. I've survived, but often just barely. I've made preposterous errors of judgment. I've made wondrously insightful "plays." I've understood, from time to time, basis economic fundamentals that should drive prices—and then don't. I've misunderstood other economic fundamentals that, in retrospect, were 180 degrees out of logic and yet prevailed profitably. I've prospered; I've almost failed utterly. I've won, I've lost, and I've broken even.

As I get older, and in my mid-50s, having seen so much of the game—for a game it is, with bad players who get lucky; great players who get unlucky; mediocre players who find their slot in the lineup and produce nice, steady results over long periods of time; "streak-y" players who score big for a while and lose big at other times—I have distilled what it is that we do to survive into a series of "Not-So-Simple" Rules of Trading that I try my best to live by every day . . . every week . . . every month. When I do stand by my rules, I prosper; when I don't, I don't. I am convinced that had Long Term Capital Management not listened to its myriad Nobel Laureates in Economics and had instead followed these rules, it would not only still be extant, it would be enormously larger, preposterously profitable, and an example to everyone. I am convinced that had Nick Leeson and Barings Brothers adhered to these rules, Barings too would be alive and functioning. Perhaps the same might even be said for Mr. Hamanaka and Sumitomo Copper.

Now, onto the Rules:

NEVER ADD TO A LOSING POSITION

RULE #1
Never, ever, under any circumstance, should one add to a losing position . . . not EVER!

Averaging down into a losing trade is the only thing that will assuredly take you out of the investment business. This is what took LTCM out. This is what took Barings Brothers out; this is what took Sumitomo Copper out, and this is what takes most losing investors out. The only thing that can happen to you when you average down into a long position (or up into a short position) is that your net worth must decline. Oh, it may turn around eventually and your decision to average down may be proven fortuitous, but for every example of fortune shining we can give an example of fortune turning bleak and deadly.

By contrast, if you buy a stock or a commodity or a currency at progressively higher prices, the only thing that can happen to your net worth is that it shall rise. Eventually, all prices tumble. Eventually, the last position you buy, at progressively higher prices, shall prove to be a loser, and it is at that point that you will have to exit your position. However, as long as you buy at higher prices, the market is telling you that you are correct in your analysis and you should continue to trade accordingly.

RULE #2
Never, ever, under any circumstance, should one add to a losing position . . . not EVER!

We trust our point is made. If "location, location, location" are the first three rules of investing in real estate, then the first two rules of trading equities, debt, commodities, currencies, and so on are these: never add to a losing position.

INVEST ON THE SIDE THAT IS WINNING

RULE #3
Learn to trade like a mercenary guerrilla.

The great Jesse Livermore once said that it is not our duty to trade upon the bullish side, nor the bearish side, but upon the winning side. This is brilliance of the first order. We must indeed learn to fight/invest on the winning side, and we must be willing to change sides immediately when one side has gained the upper hand.

Once, when Lord Keynes was appearing at a conference he had spoken to the year previous, at which he had suggested an investment in a particular stock that he was now suggesting should be shorted, a gentleman in the audience took him to task for having changed his view. This gentleman wondered how it was possible that Lord Keynes could shift in this manner and thought that Keynes was a charlatan for having changed his opinion. Lord Keynes responded in a wonderfully prescient manner when he said, *"Sir, the facts have changed regarding this company, and when the facts change, I change. What do you do, Sir?"* Lord Keynes understood the rationality of trading as a mercenary guerrilla, choosing to invest/fight upon the winning side. When the facts change, we must change. It is illogical to do otherwise.

DON'T HOLD ON TO LOSING POSITIONS

RULE #4

Capital is in two varieties: Mental and Real, and, of the two, the mental capital is the most important.

Holding on to losing positions costs *real* capital as one's account balance is depleted, but it can exhaust one's mental capital even more seriously as one holds to the losing trade, becoming more and more fearful with each passing minute, day, and week, avoiding potentially profitable trades while one nurtures the losing position.

GO WHERE THE STRENGTH IS

RULE #5

The objective of what we are after is not to buy low and to sell high, but to buy high and to sell higher, or to sell short low and to buy lower.

We can never know what price is really "low," nor what price is really "high." We can, however, have a modest chance at knowing what the trend is and acting on that trend. We can buy higher and we can sell higher still if the trend is up. Conversely, we can sell short at low prices and we can cover at lower prices if the trend is still down. However, we've no idea how high high is, nor how low low is.

Nortel went from approximately the split-adjusted price of $1 share back in the early 1980s, to just under $90/share in early 2000 and back to near $1 share by 2002 (where it has hovered ever since). On the way up, it looked expensive at $20, at $30, at $70, and at $85, and on the way down it may have looked inexpensive at $70, and $30, and $20—and even at $10 and $5. The lesson here is that we really cannot tell what is high and/or what is low, but when the trend becomes established, it can run much farther than the most optimistic or most pessimistic among us can foresee.

RULE #6

Sell markets that show the greatest weakness; buy markets that show the greatest strength.

Metaphorically, when bearish we need to throw our rocks into the wettest paper sack for it will break the most readily, while in bull markets we need to ride the strongest wind for it shall carry us farther than others.

Those in the women's apparel business understand this rule better than others, for when they carry an inventory of various dresses and designers they watch which designer's work moves off the shelf most readily and which does not. They instinctively mark down the work of those designers who sell poorly, recovering what capital they can as swiftly as they can, and use that capital to buy more works by the successful designer. To do otherwise is counterintuitive. They instinctively buy the "strongest" designers and sell the "weakest." Investors in stocks all too often, and by contrast, watch their portfolio shift over time and sell out the best stocks, often deploying this capital into the shares that have lagged. They are, in essence, selling the best designers while buying more of the worst. A clothing shop owner would never do this; stock investors do it all the time and think they are wise for doing so!

MAKING "LOGICAL" PLAYS IS COSTLY

RULE #7
In a bull market we can only be long or neutral; in a bear market we can only be bearish or neutral.

Rule 6 addresses what might seem like a logical play: selling out of a long position after a sharp rush higher or covering a short position after a sharp break lower—and then trying to play the market from the other direction, hoping to profit from the supposedly inevitable correction, only to see the market continue on in the original direction that we had gotten ourselves exposed to. At this point, we are not only losing real capital, we are losing mental capital at an explosive rate, and we are bound to make more and more errors of judgment along the way.

Actually, in a bull market we can be neutral, modestly long, or aggressively long—getting into the last position after a protracted bull run into which we've added to our winning position all along the way. Conversely, in a bear market we can be neutral, modestly short, or aggressively short, but never, ever can we—or should we—be the opposite way even so slightly.

Many years ago I was standing on the top step of the CBOT bond-trading pit with an old friend, Bradley Rotter, looking down into the tumult below in awe. When asked what he thought, Brad replied, "I'm flat . . . and I'm nervous." That, we think, says it all . . . that the markets are often so terrifying that no position is a position of consequence.

RULE #8

"Markets can remain illogical far longer than you or I can remain solvent."

I understand that it was Lord Keynes who said this first, but the first time I heard it was one morning many years ago when talking with a very good friend and mentor, Dr. A. Gary Shilling, as he worried over a position in U.S. debt that was going against him and seemed to go against the most obvious economic fundamentals at the time. Worried about his losing position and obviously dismayed by it, Gary said over the phone, "Dennis, the markets are illogical at times, and they can remain illogical far longer than you or I can remain solvent." The University of Chicago "boys" have argued for decades that the markets are rational, but we in the markets every day know otherwise. We must learn to accept that irrationality, deal with it, and move on. There is not much else one can say. (Dr. Shilling's position shortly thereafter proved to have been wise and profitable, but not before further "mental" capital was expended.)

RULE #9

Trading runs in cycles; some are good, some are bad, and there is nothing we can do about that other than accept it and act accordingly.

The academics will never understand this, but those of us who trade for a living know that there are times when every trade we make (even the errors) is profitable and there is nothing we can do to change that. Conversely, there are times that no matter what we do— no matter how wise and considered are our insights; no matter how sophisticated our analysis—our trades will surrender nothing other than losses. Thus, when things are going well, trade often, trade large, and try to maximize the good fortune that is being bestowed upon you. However, when trading poorly, trade infrequently, trade very small, and continue to get steadily smaller until the winds have changed and the trading "gods" have chosen to smile upon you once again. The latter usually happens when we begin following the rules of trading again. Funny how that happens!

THINK LIKE A FUNDAMENTALIST; TRADE LIKE A TECHNICIAN

RULE #10

To trade/invest successfully, think like a fundamentalist; trade like a technician.

It is obviously imperative that we understand the economic fundamentals that will drive a market higher or lower, but we must understand the *technicals* as well. When we do, then and only then can we, or should we, trade. If the market fundamentals as we understand them are bullish and the trend is down, it is illogical to buy; conversely, if the fundamentals as we understand them are bearish but the market's trend is up, it is illogical to sell that market short. Ah, but if we understand the market's fundamentals to be bullish and if the trend is up, it is even more illogical *not* to trade bullishly.

RULE #11

Keep your technical systems simple.

Over the years we have listened to inordinately bright young men and women explain the most complicated and clearly sophisticated trading systems. These are systems that they have labored over, nurtured, expended huge sums of money and time upon, but our history has shown that they rarely make money for those employing them. Complexity breeds confusion; simplicity breeds an ability to make decisions swiftly, and to admit error when wrong. Simplicity breeds elegance.

The greatest traders/investors we've had the honor to know over the years continue to employ the simplest trading schemes. They draw simple trend lines, they see and act on simple technical signals, they react swiftly, and they attribute it to their knowledge gained over the years that complexity is the home of the young and untested.

UNDERSTAND THE ENVIRONMENT

RULE #12
In trading/investing, an understanding of mass psychology is often more important than an understanding of economics.

Markets are, as we like to say, the sum total of the wisdom and stupidity of all who trade in them, and they are collectively given over to the most basic components of the collective psychology. The dot-com bubble was indeed a bubble, but it grew from a small group to a larger group to the largest group, collectively fed by mass mania, until it ended. The economists among us missed the bull-run entirely, but that proves only that markets can indeed remain irrational, and that economic fundamentals may eventually hold the day but in the interim, psychology holds the moment.

And finally the most important rule of all:

THE RULE THAT SUMS UP THE REST

RULE #13
Do more of that which is working and do less of that which is not.

This is a simple rule in writing; this is a difficult rule to act upon. However, it synthesizes all the modest wisdom we've accumulated over thirty years of watching and trading in markets. Adding to a winning trade while cutting back on losing trades is the one true rule that holds—and it holds in life as well as in trading/investing.

If you would go to the golf course to play a tournament and find at the practice tee that you are hitting the ball with a slight "left-to-right" tendency that day, it would be best to take that notion out to the course rather than attempt to re-work your swing. Doing more of what is working works on the golf course, and it works in investing.

If you find that writing thank-you notes, following the niceties of life that are extended to you, gets you more niceties in the future, you should write more thank-you notes. If you find that being pleasant to those around you elicits more pleasantness, then be more pleasant.

And if you find that cutting losses while letting profits run—or even more directly, that cutting losses and adding to winning trades—works best of all, then that is the course of action you must take when trading/investing. Here in our offices, as we trade for our own account, we constantly ask each other, "What's working today, and what's not?" Then we try to the very best of our ability "to do more of that which is working and less of that which is not." We've no set rule on how much more or how much less we are to do, we know only that we are to do "some" more of the former and "some" less of the latter. If our long positions are up, we look at which of those long positions is doing us the most good and we do more of that. If short positions are also up, we cut back on that which is doing us the most ill. Our process is simple.

We are certain that great—even vast—holes can and will be proven in our rules by doctoral candidates in business and economics, but we care not a whit, for they work. They've proven so through time and under pressure. We try our best to adhere to them.

This is what I have learned about the world of investing over three decades. I try each day to stand by my rules. I fail miserably at times, for I break them often, and when I do I lose money and mental capital, until such time as I return to my rules and try my very best to hold strongly to them. The losses incurred are the inevitable tithe I must make to the markets to atone for my trading sins. I accept them, and I move on, but only after vowing that "I'll never do that again."

CHAPTER 3

The Triumph of Hope over Long-Run Experience: Using Past Returns to Predict Future Performance of a Money Manager

Mark Finn is chairman of Vantage Consulting Group. He is the former chairman of the Virginia Retirement System Investment Advisory Committee and the state of Alaska Investment Advisory Committee and has a distinguished investment career. He consults with large pension funds and high-net-worth investors, as well as sits on the board of a large mutual fund family. He is also on the adjunct faculty of the College of William & Mary Graduate Business School. His specialty is finding little-known (or even start-up) managers and funding them, and he has a stellar team of researchers. His firm has probably helped launch more start-up managers than any other single group. His team is a who's who of research. Along with his son, Jonathan, who is the Chief Investment Officer at Vantage, he shows us why past performance is the most widely abused investment statistic there is. I predict that this will be the essay that will be the hardest for you to incorporate into your investment strategy, but it may be the most important! I have seen more investors lose money or make mistakes using past performance than any other one single thing. Read this one over and over.

Mark is an avid golfer and Jon a competitive sailor. They live in Virginia Beach, Virginia.   —John Mauldin

The Triumph of Hope over Long-Run Experience: Using Past Returns to Predict Future Performance of a Money Manager

by Mark T. Finn and Jonathan Finn, CFA

⌒

"The path of least resistance and least trouble is a mental rut already made. It requires troublesome work to undertake the alternation of old beliefs. Self-conceit often regards it as a sign of weakness to admit that a belief to which we have once committed ourselves is wrong. We get so identified with an idea that it is literally a 'pet' notion and we rise to its defense and stop our eyes and ears to anything different."

—John Dewey

THE PATH OF LEAST RESISTANCE THAT MANY PEOPLE TAKE WHEN MAKING THE decision to invest with a money manager is to choose the one with the best track record. We do this despite the fact that "past performance may not be predictive of future returns" is a well-known phrase plastered all over the marketing material of every SEC-registered investment adviser. Yet people do not act in a manner consistent with this mandated disclosure. Our observation is that past performance dominates investors' decision processes so much that we contend that past performance data may be the most misused information in the investment business.

Performance measurement *can* be useful in understanding the sources of a manager's performance and in comparing a manager to a peer group or benchmark. However, this is a process of explanation of how the manager achieved past success (or lack thereof), not prediction, and is not the same thing as relying on past performance to predict future performance. Unfortunately, in practice, decision makers overweight historical returns in the decision equation. Sadly, they continue to repeat this mistake time after time, despite bad outcomes. We call this *the triumph of irrational hope over long-run experience.* Past performance may contain some information useful for prediction, but almost certainly not in its raw, reported form. If only life were that simple!

The reasons that life is *not* that simple are many, and their exploration is beyond the scope of this chapter. However, in the pages that follow we'll frame problems associated with the data (manager returns) and offer a simple model of investor thought processes that may help to clarify the issue.

IDENTIFYING NOISE IN MARKET DECISION MAKING

The data problem can be thought of as analogous to an engineering concept called the *signal to noise ratio.* This statistic measures the ratio of radio signals received relative to the noise that is created by the receiving system. The analogy to investing would be the ratio of the return caused by a manager's actions relative to the return caused by events and factors that were independent of the manager's decisions (*noise*). The reality is that there is a tremendous amount of variability, or noise, in security and manager returns.

What causes this variability? There are three main components:

1. *Systematic risk:* what happens to the overall stock market
2. *Residual common factor risk:* what happens to subgroups such as industries
3. *Residual specific risk:* what happens to a particular stock

For each component there are literally hundreds, or perhaps thousands, of factors, each with differing impact in different time periods. Even if one had a best guess for each factor, there still would be uncertainty or variability around that best guess. *The reality is that what an investor "knows" about the future is small compared to what he can't know.* This simple concept is so important it is worth repeating. What we know about the future is tiny compared to what we do not—and in all likelihood cannot—know. Many of the most widely accepted theories in modern finance make simplifying assumptions that discount the tremendous uncertainty of potential future events. We believe the next revolution in finance theory will be in the area of more accurately recognizing and modeling uncertainty.

This distinction between what is known and unknown is further compounded by the likelihood that information about the future that is known by one investor might also be known by other investors. To the extent the information is known by other investors, it should already be reflected in the price of the stock. Thus, if the anticipated event occurs as expected, it will not cause the price to change. The uncertainty or variability in asset returns is caused by information or events that are *not* correctly anticipated by investors.

DEALING WITH THE NOISE PROBLEM

The problem of noise has been around for a long time. How have investors dealt with this issue in the past? At first, they didn't. They tried to compare a specific manager to some broad benchmark such as the S&P 500, with the presumption that all portfolios were as diversified and as risky as the S&P 500. This was clearly not the case for many managers.

Well, if there were too many different portfolio risk levels to compare them to one market benchmark, perhaps there was another way. The next attempt focused on comparing a manager to a universe of similar managers. It was hoped that similarity in presumed client objectives would mean that the risk of the portfolios might be similar. Unfortunately this peer group idea, while having intuitive appeal, is fraught with problems.

In the 1970s the focus of risk measurement became "beta." Beta measures the sensitivity of an investment relative to some appropriate benchmark. Because of the risk-canceling benefits of diversification when you combine, say, fifty stocks across different industries into a portfolio, the portion of the portfolio's risk that is attributable to specific stock risk is reduced from roughly 50 percent to approximately 4 percent. The dominant element of risk becomes systematic risk. This systematic risk, or market risk, is the element that beta measures.

However, a key problem with beta (and there are several problems) is that it assumes all portfolios are diversified or that any common factor emphasis within a portfolio won't matter over the longer run. Evidence has shown that assumption to be quite inappropriate. Indeed, even small biases toward or away from some common factors have a major impact on performance. It turns out that these common factors are often equated with a manager's style; growth versus value, large-capitalization companies versus small, high-tech versus cyclical, and so on.[1]

This understanding has led to an emphasis on defining the most refined benchmark possible to measure a given manager. The more accurate the benchmark is in reflecting the manager's habitat or style, the more accurate will be the measure of his skill. By comparing apples to apples you reduce a significant amount of noise. This can be seen in the following illustration.

Assume that in a typical year Manager A had the monthly portfolio returns listed in Table 3.1. Also for that same period, the S&P 500 had the returns shown in Column 2 and the Russell Small Cap Index had the returns listed in the third column. The active return for Manager A versus the S&P 500 is shown in Column 4, and the active return relative to the Russell Small Cap Index is listed in Column 5.

Notice that the annualized active return relative to both the S&P 500 and the Russell Small Cap Index are identical: 3.9 percent. However, Manager A's portfolio tracks much more closely to the Russell Small Cap Index. This can be seen in the fact that the standard deviation of the active return relative to the Russell Small Cap Index is only 5.0 percent, compared to 10.0 percent relative to the

TABLE 3.1

Sample Monthly Portfolio Returns: S&P versus Russell Small Cap

	Manager A	S&P 500	Russell Small Cape		Manager A vs. S&P 500	Manager A vs. Russell Small Cap
Jan.	2.1	2.5	−0.1		−4.6	−2.0
Feb.	3.3	0.7	3.1		2.6	0.2
March	2.5	0.7	2.1		1.8	0.4
April	4.2	1.1	5.4		3.1	−1.2
May	4.1	1.9	3.9		2.2	0.1
June	−2.0	0.3	−4.1		−2.3	2.1
July	−6.7	−3.2	−8.7		−3.4	2.1
Aug.	4.5	1.5	5.8		2.9	−1.4
Sept.	3.5	4.1	3.9		−0.6	−0.4
Oct.	1.1	2.0	−1.5		−0.9	2.7
Nov.	4.0	5.5	4.1		−1.5	−0.1
Dec.	3.0	−1.4	2.6		4.4	0.4
Annualized return	20.4	16.5	16.5	Annualized active return	3.9	3.9
				Standard deviation	10.0	5.0
				Years to 5 percent statistical significance	26.1	6.6

S&P 500. This is not surprising because Manager A is a small-cap manager. What is surprising is that because of that difference in standard deviation, it would only take 6.6 years to reach statistical significance when Manager A is compared to the Russell Small Cap Index, versus 26.1 years when Manager A is compared to the S&P 500. The wrong benchmark can make a big difference in demonstrating whether a manager has skill or not!

A more sophisticated performance measure, referred to as an *information ratio*, takes into account both return and risk in one measure. The information ratio indicates the level of return obtained per unit of risk.[2] The more positive the ratio, the more skill is demonstrated.[3] A more widely used variant of the information ratio is the *Sharpe ratio*, which measures excess return per unit of risk.[4] The Sharpe ratio can be a useful way to compare the skill of two or more different investment managers who employ different strategies to earn different returns and take different levels of risk.

At the end of the day, what we find is that it takes an inordinately long time to determine if a manager's risk adjusted returns are a reflection of skill or simply luck (noise).[5] Using just the past few years of a manager's returns is pointless from a statistical point of view.

PERFORMANCE STUDIES

What do the studies show about whether past performance is predictive? The overwhelming evidence is that it is not.

First we would like to provide a brief history of these studies to give you some perspective. Most of the early studies looked at the performance of mutual funds since data for those funds were most readily available. (Later on, data from pension and endowment funds were also used.) The studies focused on a key issue: Did managers as a group outperform the market? In any large group of managers, you would expect a certain percentage of them to outperform and a certain percentage to underperform due to random fluctuations (noise). A key question was: Did the group of managers, on average, outperform the market? The answer was no. That is, professional investors as a group did not exhibit superior performance to the overall market of all investors. The next question: Was the percentage of managers that did outperform the market greater than you would expect by chance? The answer for the most part was again no. Of course this doesn't mean there couldn't be a superior manager within this subset. Our conclusion is that you couldn't identify him or her by using past performance.

Also, most of the early performance studies were subject to a key defect: *survivor bias*. Survivor bias is caused when you focus on managers that had data for an entire period. Those managers that went out of business or merged often were dropped out of the sample. Since this subset of managers was most likely to have had the worst performance, the results were biased upward.

Since it is more difficult to measure each manager relative to his own custom benchmark (i.e., a small-cap value manager against the Russell 2000 Value Index) than just the market as a whole, many studies just compared managers to the performance of the S&P 500 or NYSE.

One study that did a good job of measuring managers against the proper benchmark was conducted by Ronald Kahn and Andrew Rudd.[6] After adjusting for style, the authors found that past performance had no correlation with future performance for the equity managers studied.

REASONS PAST PERFORMANCE FAILS AS AN INVESTING TOOL

Past performance is useful in explaining why a manager performed the way he did during a specific period. This is called *performance attribution*. Performance attribution can tell you what portion of the portfolio's return could be attributed to its different industry selections, what portion was attributed to the beta or systematic risk level, what portion was due to different exposures to common factors such as size, and what portion could be attributed to stock selection. However, knowing where the performance came from is not the same as predicting where and at what level it will come from in the future.

We already discussed noise as a key contributor to the failure of past performance data as an investment decision tool, but we would be remiss if we didn't mention a few other reasons past performance is not predictive.

First there is the problem of the performance of a portfolio versus the performance of a specific fund manager. Turnover in the investment management team that has produced the past performance record will minimize the usefulness of that record.

Another more subtle but nonetheless very real problem in analyzing past performance studies is the weighting given to each manager. Most studies weight each manager in the study equally. That may tell you what the average manager has done, but it doesn't tell you anything about how the typical client has done. The largest mutual funds may manage hundreds of times as many assets as the average money manager, and their performance would consequently affect a larger number of investors. We must be careful in drawing conclusions about how well clients have fared because client assets are not distributed equally among all investment managers.

There is also the problem of time period. In the past it was assumed that any five-year period would encompass both a bull and a bear market. This is, however, a very naive assumption. Even if a past track record includes an up and a down market period, that still might not be good enough. After all, there are different factors at work that produce each up and down market. Just because a manager may have made good decisions in one set of economic circumstances doesn't mean he will be able to perform as well in a different economic environment. The divergent performance of growth managers before and after the bursting of the technology bubble is a noteworthy example.

Also for those of us who tend to the cynical side, there are two additional problems with past performance. Often, smaller managers who are trying to get big will make bigger bets earlier in the life of their firm. As assets come in and revenues increase, the managers become more interested in not losing the assets they have, so they tend to become more conservative.

Even if that wasn't a conscious decision, it is sometimes the case that a manager who can effectively manage $500 million can't apply those skills as effectively managing $5 billion.

Finally, this is a competitive business. If a manager has found a technique that works (such as earnings surprise or insider trading), there will be a tendency for other managers to want to use those same techniques, and if enough of them do so, the advantage will be arbitraged away.

The whole issue of past performance might be amusing if it didn't lead to some tragic consequences. Let us give you some examples.

Few people will hire a manager with a sub-par performance record. Indeed, performance is often the first and most important screen used to select managers. We have seen plan sponsors look only at managers that were in the top quartile over the last five years. However, if a common factor has been especially important over that five-year period, then there will be a disproportionate number of managers who made it to the top quartile simply because they had an above average exposure to that factor. While the manager should get credit if he intentionally raised his exposure to that factor in anticipation of its positive impact, that isn't usually the case. More often, the manager has a style or habitat that he or she feels comfortable with. Remember, 90 percent of a manager's differential performance can be ascribed to the manager's style. If you are a value manager when value stocks are doing well, you will have a great performance advantage over other managers who are not selecting stocks within the value style.

Figure 3.1 shows the relative performance of value stocks versus growth stocks. The black line represents the cumulative 12-month rolling performance of value stocks less the performance of all stocks. When the line is above zero, value stocks are outperforming the overall market and vice versa. The performance of growth stocks, after subtracting the performance of all stocks, is shown in gray. As can be seen, there are significant periods of time when growth stocks do well relative to the overall market, and value stocks tend not to do as well. In those periods when growth stocks are doing well, any manager who has growth stocks as his or her habitat will have a tremendous performance advantage relative to any value manager. As the graph illustrates, the performance differentials can be significant and they can reverse sharply. As an aside, new research that the performance differential attributed to this so-called *value effect* may in fact also explain a significant portion of the *size effect* (small vs. large-cap) is forcing the industry to more closely examine style issues. The fact is that the majority of investors who decided to invest in growth managers in the latter part of 1999 because of a solid five-year track record of superior performance got a painful reminder that past performance is not predictive.

By using past performance as a criteria for selection, investors often unwittingly introduce a bias into their portfolio. We know one

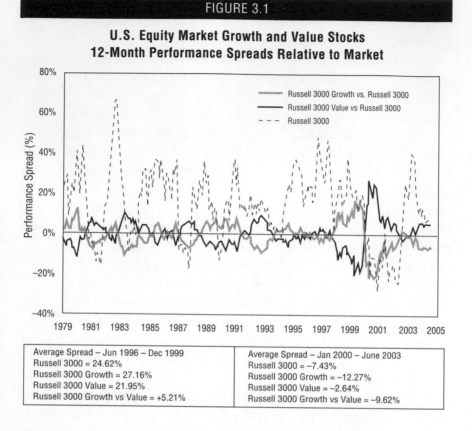

FIGURE 3.1

U.S. Equity Market Growth and Value Stocks
12-Month Performance Spreads Relative to Market

Average Spread – Jun 1996 – Dec 1999	Average Spread – Jan 2000 – June 2003
Russell 3000 = 24.62%	Russell 3000 = –7.43%
Russell 3000 Growth = 27.16%	Russell 3000 Growth = –12.27%
Russell 3000 Value = 21.95%	Russell 3000 Value = –2.64%
Russell 3000 Growth vs Value = +5.21%	Russell 3000 Growth vs Value = –9.62%

institution that hired an entire new line-up of managers. Because of the reliance on a past performance screen (selecting only managers with top quartile performance), they incorporated a strong bias in their composite portfolio. The decision makers at this institution thought they were being careful by making sure they selected from the best growth versus value and small versus large cap managers in their candidate universe. However, over the three years prior to their investment decision, stocks with high trading momentum had done especially well. This is unusual because this characteristic had resulted in sub-par performance on average over the previous thirty years! We would argue that this institution has an unconscious and big bet on high trading/turnover stocks continuing to do well, since many of the new managers the institution hired shared that common characteristic. Indeed, one could postulate that those same managers wound up in the top quartile precisely because they had that exposure.

The fact is that relying on past performance can often introduce biases into a portfolio that you neither know of nor want.

WHY DO INVESTORS RELY ON PAST PERFORMANCE?

Studies have shown that even managers with the best long-term records commonly underperform the market 40 percent of the time, and it is not unusual for them to have periods of three to five years of sub-par performance. Why do investors assume past performance is predictive? A big factor is our lack of appreciation of the level of uncertainty and the central role uncertainty plays in just about everything related to investing. Most of us focus on trying to understand or explain why a particular event occurred. We spend little effort gathering all the possible scenarios before the fact. In general, people feel uncomfortable dealing with uncertainty. After all, uncertainty is directly related to the degree of control we have in our own lives. It is also directly related to how much we know. The less we know about different factors, causation, relationship, and so on, the more uncertainty there is. Indeed, predicting is based on one's causal understanding of how the world works. It can be very discouraging to realize how limited is our understanding of cause and effect.

Couple this natural discomfort and uncertainty with hindsight bias and you have the ingredients for self-delusion. Essentially, hindsight bias is the group of distortions that are created when we have knowledge of an event that has already occurred. When we remember the past, we find it almost impossible to remember the full range of uncertainties facing us at the time. Rather, we remember a reconstruction of past events in terms of what actually happened. This makes what happened seem much more inevitable than it actually was. Thus, if we know a manager has had a certain performance record, we will also selectively remember all the facts that were available at the time that would support the link between the manager's actions and that performance record. This will result in the impression that past performance data are more predictive than they actually are.

Two additional factors may be at work here. First, we (in the Western World in particular) have been educated in a framework best described by reference to Sir Isaac Newton. This is a world of cause and effect. We believe that things are connected in a causal way, and when we see an outcome we naturally tend to attribute a cause. Second, the information processing limitations of the human mind may contribute to our tendency to overweight historical performance. Our minds have evolved shortcuts designed to simplify our lives. The old saying, "If it looks like a duck and quacks like a duck, then it must be a duck," is an example. The problem is that a bad manager can have good numbers—look and sound good—just by random luck.

Finally, a number of studies in behavioral finance have shown that accuracy does not improve linearly (one for one) with the amount of information used to reach a decision. However, humans tend to act in a manner consistent with the view that the more information we consider the more accurate our conclusion will be. This relationship is captured by the confidence expressed by subjects during testing. Studies have shown a nearly one-to-one relationship between the amount of information people have about a problem and the degree of confidence they have in their solution. In experiments where participants were required to make a decision as each new piece of information was revealed, the accuracy of their decision did not increase with new information, only their confidence in their decision. Why is this important? Because when we are looking for data points to base our investment decision on, we too often rely on the most accessible and readily available data we can find—past performance. Although this past performance information may help us feel better about our decision, it does not make us better decision makers. In this case we would argue that it makes us more likely to choose an investment manager that has been lucky, but has no real skill, because we have in fact deluded ourselves rather than searching for the clues to skill that really matter.

In summary, people have great difficulty in dealing with the randomness that abounds in the real world. They want to believe the world is more predictable than it is. Many studies document this tendency. (For an example, see the classic studies done by W.A. Wagenaar in Acta Psychologica.)

HOW SHOULD YOU USE PERFORMANCE DATA?

There is a branch of probability theory that offers some useful insights into how to integrate different sources of information when making predictions. It is called *Bayesian statistics.* In assessing an investment manager's ability (and hence likelihood of producing superior future performance), there are three sources of information.

First is one's prior belief as to the range of abilities across active managers in general. What would the range of alphas be so that two-thirds of all managers' alphas will fall within that range? The more one believed in efficient markets, the more likely one would estimate the average alpha to be negative (because of fees and transaction costs). Also, a believer in efficient markets would think there was very little range of true alphas around that negative average alpha. As a reference point, informal surveys done with groups of professional investment managers showed that they thought the average manager would produce a zero alpha and that two-thirds of all managers would fall within −2 percent to +2 percent alpha.

The next source of information is one's belief as to a manager's alpha based on an in-depth understanding of the people, process, and philosophy employed by that manager. In other words, this source of information is any information about that particular manager independent of historical performance. With access to all this non-past performance information, what do you think the chances are that you would mistakenly conclude that an average or unskillful manager was actually a superior/skillful manager? Again, as a point of reference, surveys of professional investors showed that the standard deviation of their estimate was 1.5 percent. That is, professional investors had a fair degree of confidence in their ability to analyze the likely skill of a money manager independent of past performance data.

The final source of information is the historical performance record of a manager. Let us assume for illustrative purposes that a particular manager produced a positive alpha relative to his or her benchmark of 3.0 percent with a standard deviation of 6 percent over the last five years.

How should we incorporate all this information? Based on the numbers provided by surveys of professional investors, how much weight should one give to past performance? Bayesian statistics can calculate an answer. The results are that prior beliefs about the range of skill of money managers in general should get a 35 percent weight. Information about the particular money manager excluding past performance data should get a 61 percent weight. Past performance should get only a 4 percent weight.[7]

You can substitute your own assumptions, but we doubt whether any reasonable assumptions would justify the overwhelming weight commonly given past performance when people try to predict a manager's future performance. Under most reasonable assumptions, we would guess that the most important source of information when predicting future performance would be external information about the particular manager, exclusive of past performance.

However, evaluating this source of information is a very complex and subtle topic in its own right. Suffice it to say that manager analysis is a very intense and time-consuming process.

There are a few situations where past performance may be predictive of future performance. These situations arise when several criteria are met:

1. The benchmark is a very good representation of all aspects of the manager's style or habitat.
2. The performance record is the result of many decisions made over many different market environments.
3. Either the portfolio is well diversified or the manager specified in advance why certain investment decisions would result in superior performance.
4. The regime in which the manager was operating does not radically change and the manager produced an alpha that was large relative to the portfolio's level of diversification.

However, situations where these criteria hold are quite rare and involve uncertainty in their own right (i.e., regime change). Indeed, they are so rare that past performance in most cases is useless in predicting future performance. Believing otherwise can be very dangerous to your financial health. Unfortunately that is how most people, even those who know better, weight their decision calculus—thus our claim that past performance is the most misused information in the investment business.

In conclusion, we recommend the following:

- Look hard at all the risks associated with estimating information ratios.
- Bring into the decision equation all the information on the manager's process you can.
- Factor measurable beta out of historic performance, while relentlessly searching for uncorrelated strategies.
- Use a Bayesian approach.
- Dampen your enthusiasm and let common sense and experience play an important role in the decision process.

When the time comes to put the portfolio together, weight the allocation to your various managers by the inverse of their variance (or volatility). This is called *volatility throttling*. In other words, take their volatility and weight your allocation to them by the inverse of the volatility (one over their volatility). This means the lower-volatility managers will get more of your portfolio because they probably have less noise in their particular portfolio management style. In essence, this will tend to dampen the noise in your personal portfolio.

But remember, past performance is about hope. We *hope* that the manager will deliver those great returns to us going forward, but as a wise man once said, "Hope is a good companion but a poor guide."

CHAPTER 4

The Long Bond

⌒

Most of us were first introduced to A. Gary Shilling through
Forbes, *where he has been a columnist for more than twenty
years. He made his reputation with a number of outstanding calls
early in his career. In the spring of 1969, he was among the few
who correctly saw that a recession would start late in that year.
In 1973, he stood almost alone in forecasting that the world was
entering a massive inventory-building spree, to be followed by the
first major worldwide recession since the 1930s. In the late 1970s,
when most people thought that raging inflation would last
forever, Shilling was the first to predict that the changing political
mood of the country would lead to an end of severe inflation, as
well as to potentially serious financial and economic
readjustment problems, and a shift in investment strategy from
one favoring tangible assets to emphasis on stocks and bonds.
Subsequently, he has become known as "Doctor Disinflation." The*
Wall Street Journal *once noted that among economists predicting
bond rates, Shilling had the best track record. Gary is well known
for his forecasting record.*

*And he has kept that track record going. When almost no one
agreed with him, he wrote the definitive book titled* Deflation *in
1998, which accurately predicted the continued move toward far
lower inflation and to what Gary thinks will ultimately be a good
deflation of 1 to 2 percent.*

This chapter discusses the right way to evaluate investment themes. You should look for the large out-of-consensus calls as the way to grow your capital, and Gary tells us how to spot those calls.   —John Mauldin

The Long Bond

by A. Gary Shilling, Ph.D.

FIND AN IMPORTANT, *NONCONSENSUS* AND LONG-TERM INVESTMENT THEME—
and stick with it. That's the most important thing I've learned from
38 years in the economic consulting and investment business.

INVESTMENTS MUST MAKE MONEY

To be useful, an investment theme must have the potential to make
serious money. This may seem intuitively obvious, but it isn't to
many economists. Years ago, the chief economist at a major mutual
fund and investment advisory firm was visiting me in our offices
when the latest quarterly GDP numbers were announced. He was
very upset because his forecast was off the mark by 0.2 percentage
points, and he spent half an hour poring over the GDP components
and repeatedly telling me that he couldn't understand why he wasn't
right on the money. At no point did he express any interest in what
these numbers might mean for stocks, bonds, or other investments.
I tried to introduce a note of reality by asking him on which exchange GDP traded, but he only responded with a quizzical look.

This chief economist is not alone—at least to the extent that
forecasting accuracy reflects the emphasis that forecasters put on
the various series they try to prognosticate. A study of the *Wall
Street Journal*'s semi-annual poll of economists found that their
forecasts of inflation six months hence were better than the assumptions of no change in the inflation rate. So far, so good. But
their translations of those inflation forecasts into interest rate predictions were disastrous. Taking the exact opposite position from
that poll's average forecast of the change in the thirty-year Treasury

bond yield, semester-by-semester, would have produced double-digit returns.

BE NONCONSENSUS AND LONG-TERM

A useful investment theme must also be *nonconsensus*. With today's widespread and instantly available information, the consensus view is fully reflected, or *discounted*, by security markets. If the vast majority of pundits expects overall corporate earnings to be up 10 percent in a given quarter, stocks won't move much if that forecast does, in fact, turn out to be true. Only a correct forecast of, say, a 20 percent gain adds any value because when it is realized, equities will move appreciably.

An investment theme must also be valid for many years to be highly successful for most investors. Sure, skilled day traders can profit handsomely from short-term themes, but for the rest, random market fluctuations make even correct ideas difficult to implement, and they will likely be old hat before most investors take action. A correct forecast of unexpected weakness in payroll employment in a particular month would probably spur Treasury bond prices, but the gains might erode quickly if the weekly jobless benefit claims in succeeding weeks were well below the consensus forecasts.

THE LATE 1970s

In the late 1970s, I developed an important, nonconsensus, and long-term investment theme that has worked well ever since. At that time, inflation was leaping and most observers believed it would persist forever (see Figure 4.1). As usual, theory followed fact, and several were concocted to explain chronic inflation. Furthermore, surging prices of crude oil and other commodities, wages, and almost everything else made these constructs very credible to many.

One especially potent theory was that in democracies with universal suffrage, the numerous low-income voters will demand and get more and more government programs that benefited them, fi-

FIGURE 4.1

Consumer Price Index (monthly year/year % change)

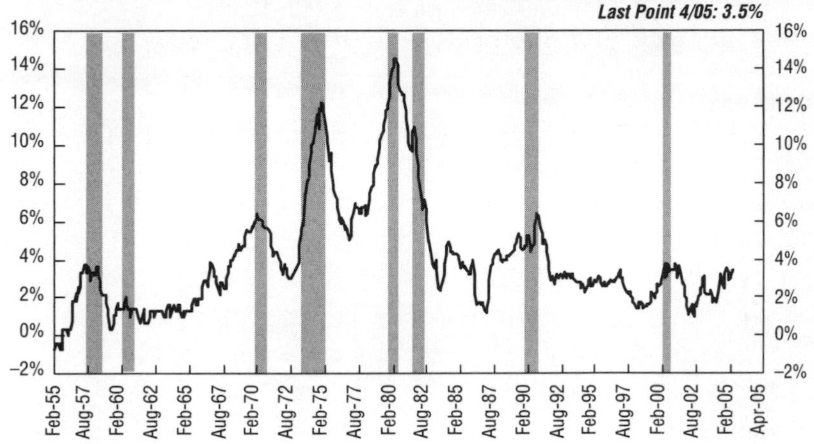

Last Point 4/05: 3.5%

Shaded areas are recessions.

Source: Bureau of Labor Statistics

nanced by soaking the rich but also by the inflation-inducing printing of money. So, the only solution was the gold standard, under which gold is the basis of the money supply. That, the theory went, would limit the creation of credit and curtail inflation. This view was proclaimed loudly by a number of leading businessmen and academics.

In contrast, we were convinced that the root of inflation was simply excessive spending that pushed overall demand above aggregate supply. Furthermore, the national government is the only economic sector with good enough credit to finance and continue chronic, substantial overspending. These conditions normally occur in shooting wars, but the overspending was just as meaningful in the Cold War then in progress, augmented by War on Poverty spending.

MONETARY OR FISCAL POLICY?

Many, of course, argue that inflation is always and everywhere a monetary phenomenon. Excessive credit creates the inflation-generating

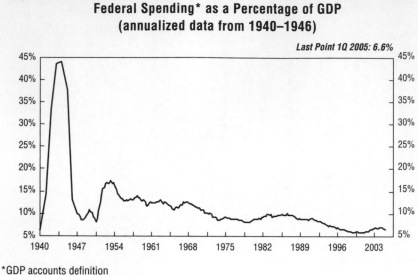

FIGURE 4.2

**Federal Spending* as a Percentage of GDP
(annualized data from 1940–1946)**

Last Point 1Q 2005: 6.6%

*GDP accounts definition
Source: Bureau of Economic Analysis

excessive demand. That may be true in a direct sense, but it doesn't mean that monetary policy is the prime mover. If it were, you'd conclude that the Fed in the 1941 to 1945 years was inhabited by people who idiotically mushroomed the money supply and guaranteed rampant inflation once wartime price and wage controls were removed.

In fact, excessive government outlays were the fundamental factor. In order to encourage support for the war effort, the federal government did not raise taxes enough to offset the jump in military and, therefore, total government spending (see Figure 4.2). So, the huge gap was bridged by patriotic purchases of war bonds and the leap in the money supply (see Figure 4.3). Obviously, government spending was the prime mover, and monetary policy was merely its handmaiden.

DISTRUST IN GOVERNMENT

In any event, it was clear to me in the late 1970s that the frustrations over Vietnam and the failures of the Great Society programs, as well

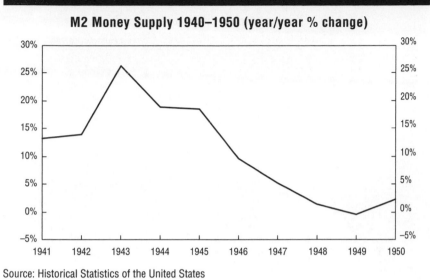

FIGURE 4.3

M2 Money Supply 1940–1950 (year/year % change)

Source: Historical Statistics of the United States

as Watergate, had turned the electorate against Washington. This was a complete flip-flop from the earlier near-complete trust in government, the culmination of the long liberal swing that started in 1933. By the 1960s, many believed Administration economists when they said they were so skillful in implementing monetary and fiscal policy that they could prevent minor economic dips as well as major recessions. Also credible was the Administration's contention that just a little more government spending would solve all the nation's social ills. And President Johnson convinced many that the nation could fight a land war in Asia while embarking on massive domestic spending—the guns *and* butter strategy.

MY FEARLESS FORECAST

So, in the late 1970s, long before the Cold War started to unwind, I concluded that voter pressure would curtail federal spending and we'd soon be in a long-term era of disinflation—lower and lower but still positive inflation rates. This forecast was reinforced by actions by the Fed, which had been behind the curve but finally spiked interest rates in 1979 (see Figure 4.4).

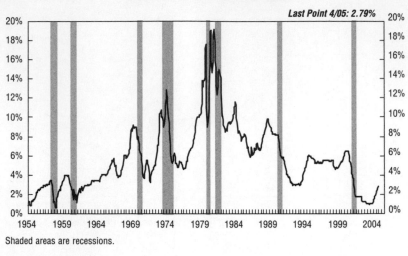

FIGURE 4.4

Federal Funds Effective Rate

Last Point 4/05: 2.79%

Shaded areas are recessions.

Source: Federal Reserve

The logical consequence of a long decline in inflation would be an equally long decline in long-term interest rates, since inflation and Treasury bond yields track closely (see Figure 4.5). So, in 1981, when Treasury bond yields reached their peak of 14.7 percent, I stated that we were entering "the bond rally of a lifetime" that would eventually reduce those yields to 4 to 5 percent. This, then, was my big long-term investment theme.

Almost no one at the time, however, took this forecast seriously. In fact, few believed that inflation could ever decline, and in the early 1980s, looked at the drops in inflation rates and Treasury yields after their tops as momentary dips. Hence the poor reception for my first book, *Is Inflation Ending? Are You Ready?*, which was written in 1982 and finally published in the spring of 1983 by McGraw-Hill.

In it, I answered the first question in the title with yes, inflation is ending due to the public's newfound distrust in government. The answer to the second question, however, was no, investors are not ready. Their portfolios were stuffed with coins, art, antiques, gold and other tangible assets that were the beneficiaries of raging infla-

FIGURE 4.5

20-year Treasury Yield and Consumer Prices

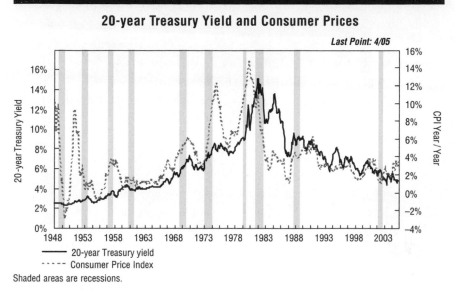

Last Point: 4/05

——— 20-year Treasury yield
- - - - - Consumer Price Index

Shaded areas are recessions.

Source: Federal Reserve and Bureau of Labor Statistics

tion. But they had far too few stocks and bonds, which would rally as inflation faded.

This forecast was decidedly nonconsensus and remained so for years, so deeply ingrained was the previous decade-and-a-half of leaping inflation and surging bond yields. Only in 1986 did our earlier predictions begin to gain credibility. That year, quite independently, the business editors of *The Boston Globe* and the *Seattle Post-Intelligencer* remembered my book, realized how its predictions were unfolding, and wrote very glowing ex post reviews of it. Well, those reviews were extremely gratifying but basically Pyrrhic victories since by 1986 *Is Inflation Ending? Are You Ready?* was long out of print.

NO STRAIGHT LINE

The decline in Treasury bond yields that commenced in November 1981 was decidedly not a straight line, and there were some hair-curling back-ups in interest rates (see Figure 4.5). My basic reasons for the long-term decline in inflation and Treasury bond yields never changed, but there were trying times. As I've said for years to myself and to anyone who will listen, markets can remain irrational a lot longer than most of us can remain solvent.

Sure, with perfect hindsight, the best strategy would have been to buy long Treasurys in 1981 and then take a vacation in the intervening 24 years on some island where there are no newspapers or securities quote machines. But that's not the real world. The buy-and-hold forever strategy is difficult to stick to and, not surprisingly, normally only comes into vogue at the end of a long run of success. That was true of stocks in the late 1990s after the lengthy and robust rally that started in August 1982 and ended with speculative extremes.

In normal times, investment positions need to be adjusted in light of current market conditions. Call it market timing if you will, but for most it's essential for investment survival. Otherwise, the risk is that investors who attempt to maintain their positions through what they hope are temporary setbacks will get scared out just at the point that markets reverse in their favor. The trick is to maintain the courage of your convictions, even if you get frightened out, and re-enter despite previous substantial losses. I certainly learned that when I first put my money where my mouth was in "the bond rally of a lifetime."

REAL MONEY

In the early 1980s, I investigated various leverage plays on 30-year Treasury bonds, and found I could leverage them in the repo market through a small bond firm owned by a friend, Edward A. Moos. Essentially, Ed bought the bonds in my account and then financed the purchase with 100 percent loans in the short-term market. I didn't put up any money, but had to cover any losses on a daily basis.

And initially there were losses. Big losses. I was stunned. I remember driving my car around town thinking, here I am, a world-class forecaster, prognosticating a major investment opportunity, and I manage to lose money on it in the first try. Am I half as smart as I thought?

But after a few weeks, I regained my composure and repeated the exercise. And with considerable success. In fact, by the mid-1980s, the result was financial independence for the Shilling family, achieved through aggressive investment in "the long bond," as the most recently issued 30-year maturity Treasury is called. The Treasury stopped issuing 30-year maturities in 2001 when forecasts of huge federal surpluses made them unnecessary. Recently, however, it decided to resume semi-annual auctions in 2006 due to the return of chronic federal deficits, the Treasury's desire to keep the average maturities of its obligations from falling, and private pension funds' newfound zeal for safe long-term investments. I'm glad because I have a very warm spot for that instrument.

THE LONG (UNLAUNCHED) BOND

I'm also sentimental about the long bond because that almost became the name of a boat. We never owned a powerboat at our beach house on Fire Island, off the south coast of Long Island, because we wanted our four kids to learn to sail and figured that a powerboat would be a big distraction. By the mid-1980s, however, the kids had become good sailors, and I was becoming increasingly frustrated by what I call the tyranny of the ferry schedule. You need to take a ferry to get to Fire Island, and I do have a chronic tendency to run late—very late. So, owning a powerboat was an attractive idea.

At the time, we were doing consulting work for CML Group, based in the Boston area and named for Charles M. Leighton, the CEO and a former professor at Harvard Business School. The firm owned a number of upscale consumer product lines, including Boston Whaler boats. I asked Charlie Leighton if I could take out some of our consulting fees in trade, specifically in the form of a Whaler. He said fine, and to let him know when I'd have a half-day free so I could visit the Whaler production facilities in Hingham, south of Boston.

We arranged a time when I was going to be in Boston anyway,

and they sent a limo to pick me up. The head of the Whaler division, Joe Lawler, and the boat's original designer, who had sold the business years earlier but was still on the payroll, personally gave me a tour of the manufacturing operation. It was interesting to see how they sprayed the fiberglass on the molds, installed floats inside the seats, and did the finishing.

Then on to the showroom. "What do you want to do with your boat?" Joe asked. I explained that I wanted to use the Whaler to get back and forth across the Great South Bay, to go fishing out in the ocean, to take the kids water skiing, etc.—in other words, I needed your all-purpose boat.

"Well, if you want to fish in the ocean, you'll need the big job over here," he said, walking toward their largest model. "And you should have two outboard engines in case one conks out thirty miles offshore with a storm brewing." We also decided that I'd need the console and windshield to hide behind in heavy weather, the built-in fish tanks, heavy-duty railings, miscellaneous storage lockers, and so on.

On the ride back to the airport in Boston, I began to wonder about the cost of *The Long Bond*, as my boat would be christened. I found out when the numbers—at Whaler's lowest wholesale prices—arrived from Joe a few days later. Then came the sharp pencil work. I figured the depreciation on the boat, the cost of the money tied up, maintenance, summer docking fees, winter storage costs, fuel, insurance, license fees, and taxes. Then I estimated how often I'd use it on fishing trips, water skiing, cruising and, of course, ferry-avoiding trips across the bay.

The results were shocking. The ferry ride cost $5 at that time, but each trip across the bay in *The Long Bond* would run $500. Now, it wasn't a matter of being able to afford the craft. This wasn't quite up to the vessel J.P. Morgan was referring to when he said that if you have to ask the price, you can't afford a yacht. I wasn't even scared off by the old definition of a boat—a hole in the water into which you pour money. I just simply couldn't justify paying a hundred times the ferry's fare for the privilege of avoiding its tyranny.

Needless to say, "The Long Bond" remains unbought—and unlaunched.

HANG IN THERE

What made my personal investment success possible, the success in other people's portfolios that we manage, and the useful recommendations I made to our economic consulting clients over many years was persistence in the face of occasional adversity and constant disbelief by others. Luckily, having a personality that's contrarian by nature is a good trait to have in my trade. Still, being comfortable, even happy, when I'm out of the mainstream can be embarrassing, especially for my wife. We'll go to a cocktail party and someone will remark, "Oh, what a beautiful yellow moon tonight!" My instinctive reply is, "What makes you think it isn't green?"

This attitude is enhanced by the ability, the result of decades of hard experience, to keep the big picture in perspective, to not get carried away with the ongoing chatter on the financial news TV channels or the seemingly important but ephemeral stories in the financial press. Bear in mind that the media offers absolutely no guidance on what's important and what isn't. No financial TV screen ever goes black for an hour after the anchor announces that they have nothing of significance to report in the next sixty minutes. No financial newspaper ever prints columns on the front page that are entirely white except for a brief notice that they have no stories that warrant front page coverage.

After the 1987 stock market crash, I, along with many others, was convinced that dire times lay ahead for equities and the economy. I spent many hours each day devouring the legions of Crash-related stories in the *Wall Street Journal* and other financial publications, and amassed huge files of clippings. We even wrote a book with the title, *After The Crash—Recession or Depression?*

Well, of course, neither recession nor depression occurred. The economy paused briefly before resuming growth, and stocks regained their upward trend in a matter of months. In retrospective, the Crash was simply a correction of the speculative leap in early 1987 and a mere blip in a robust upward trend (see Figure 4.6).

I learned from this experience. So when the 9/11 terrorist attacks occurred in 2001, I read the related news accounts but skipped lots of the details. I didn't accumulate files of press clippings. We didn't

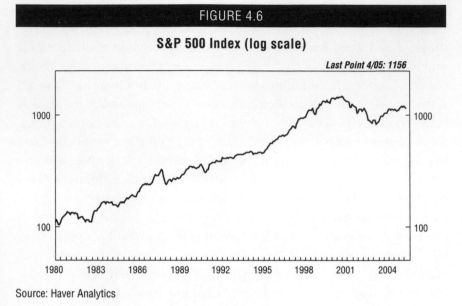

FIGURE 4.6

S&P 500 Index (log scale)

Last Point 4/05: 1156

Source: Haver Analytics

forecast huge negative effects for the economy, and didn't write a book to that effect.

CONSISTENCY IS IMPORTANT

I mentioned earlier the study of the *Wall Street Journal*'s semi-annual poll of economists that revealed their miserable record in forecasting Treasury bond yields. The *Journal* article discussing that study did go on to name "the economist with by far the best record in picking when to buy long-term bonds: A. Gary Shilling." It also said that "investors who bet on his rate forecasts by putting their money in long-term bonds did very well."

I was obviously pleased, and called up the author of the study, Robert Beckwith, then a portfolio manager at Fidelity Investments in Boston, to thank him for discussing my bond rate forecasting record. He volunteered that the reason I stood out was because I continuously forecast declining Treasury bond yields, and was never sidetracked by extraneous current issues. Others, he said, were swayed by contemporary conditions and forecast declining rates one semester and rising bond yields the next. In so doing, they missed the persistent, robust trend of declining bond yields and rising bond prices.

Indeed, I can't recall one time in this almost 24-year-old "bond rally of a lifetime" when the herd agreed with me that the trend of inflation and Treasury yields would continue down. As a result, my forecast has always been comfortably nonconsensus. It also means that Treasury bond prices have not tended to get unrealistically ahead of themselves, as is normally the case of any investment theme when most investors become true believers. Think of the ridiculous extremes of the dot-com nonsense in the late 1990s when the vast majority of stockholders believed that every IPO was destined for the heavens.

Moreover, after almost 24 years, few agree with us that inflation will go still lower—to mild deflation of 1 to 2 percent per year, and that Treasury bond yields, now 4.4 percent, will fall to 3 percent as a result. Our good friend Jim Bianco of Bianco Research notes that in that semi-annual *Wall Street Journal* poll—which I was kicked out of several years ago, probably for being bearish but correct in the early 2000s—more than 90 percent of economists have forecast higher rates since July 2002 (see Table 4.1). These expectations are unusually lopsided in the 20-year-plus history of the poll (see Figure 4.7). Similarly, the Bloomberg monthly economist survey shows that more than 90 percent have expected higher rates since December 2003. Yet Treasury bond yields have continued to fall (see Figure 4.8).

Economists are not alone. A survey conducted by another good friend, Ed Hyman at International Strategy and Investment, shows that professional bond managers since early 2002 have been shortening the durations of their portfolios in anticipation of higher yields. Yet long-bond yields have continued to fall. The yields are plotted inversely in Figure 4.9 to approximate the bond price movement. J.P. Morgan's survey of bond managers shows similar results.

Bill Gross, the bond guru at Pacific Investment Management Co. (Pimco), stated over a year ago that the two-decade-long bond rally

TABLE 4.1

The *Wall Street Journal* Forecasting Survey
(Long-term interest rate forecasts for the next six months)

Date of Survey	Forecasted Change in Yield	Actual Change in Yield	Was the Forecast in Direction Correct?	% of Respondents that Were Forecasting Long Rates to Be:		
				Higher	Lower	Unchanged
Jul 1995	−0.04%	−0.70%	YES	48%	52%	0%
Jan 1996	0.06%	0.95%	YES	56%	42%	2%
Jul 1996	−0.03%	−0.25%	YES	48%	46%	5%
Jan 1997	−0.12%	0.14%	NO	30%	70%	0%
Jul 1997	0.01%	−0.86%	NO	49%	51%	0%
Jan 1998	0.10%	−0.28%	NO	58%	42%	0%
Jul 1998	0.08%	−0.55%	NO	62%	35%	3%
Jan 1999	−0.05%	0.89%	NO	37%	54%	9%
Jul 1999	−0.15%	0.50%	NO	28%	67%	6%
Jan 2000	−0.10%	−0.58%	YES	35%	49%	15%
Jul 2000	0.11%	−0.40%	NO	61%	16%	6%
Jan 2001	−0.15%	0.30%	NO	20%	69%	11%
Jul 2001	−0.10%	−0.31%	YES	39%	59%	2%
Jan 2002	0.04%	−0.22%	NO	42%	58%	0%
Jul 2002	0.40%	−0.98%	NO	93%	7%	0%
Jan 2003	0.50%	−0.31%	NO	93%	5%	0%
Jul 2003	0.34%	0.74%	YES	87%	9%	4%
Jan 2004	0.50%	0.34%	YES	96%	4%	0%
Jul 2004	0.55%	−0.37%	NO	96%	2%	0%
Jan 2005	0.57%	??	??	98%	2%	0%

Source: Bianco Research

was over and that higher inflation and higher bond yields lay ahead. Now Pimco has $39 billion in mutual funds and institutional accounts aimed at making money if inflation jumps. These funds are invested in Treasury Inflation-Protected Securities (TIPS), which adjust for inflation to protect investors from rising inflation rates, but do not enjoy the price appreciation of conventional Treasurys when inflation and yields drop. Pimco also has invested heavily in commodities whose prices it expects to jump in renewed inflationary times. Recently, however, Gross has reversed his position and joined our camp.

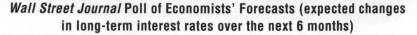

FIGURE 4.7

***Wall Street Journal* Poll of Economists' Forecasts (expected changes in long-term interest rates over the next 6 months)**

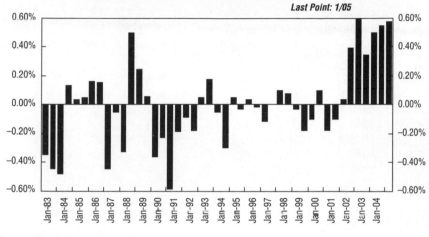

Source: Bianco Research

FIGURE 4.8

30-Year Treasury Bond Yields

Source: Ryan Labs, Inc.

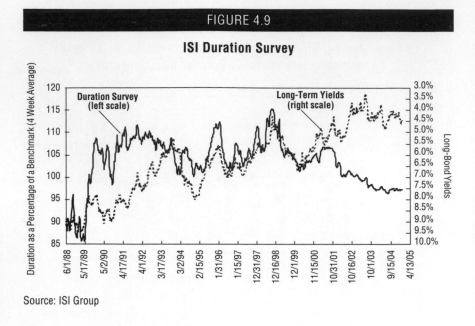

FIGURE 4.9

ISI Duration Survey

Source: ISI Group

WHY BUCK THE TREND?

To be sure, there is that slight, minuscule, remote, tiny possibility that my forecast is dead wrong and that higher inflation and a leap in Treasury bond yields lie ahead. Still, why have the vast majority of economists, individual investors, and even professional bond managers in the past bucked the 24-year trend toward lower yields? It's certainly persisted long enough to promote interest if not over-enthusiasm. Recall that the stock rally that commenced in 1982 was long enough and strong enough that about 15 years later, in the late 1990s, it sired wild and irrational exuberance.

Individual investors apparently have resisted the allure of declining bond yields because they love stocks but think they can't fathom bonds. Sure, you have to understand that since the coupon payment on an outstanding bond is fixed, the price fluctuates to adjust the market yield to current interest rates. In essence, if market rates drop from 10 to 5 percent over time, the prices of a bond with a 10 percent coupon would double to reduce the effective yield to 5 percent. So, as interest rates fall, bond prices rise. But is this such a difficult concept?

Beyond this interest rate volatility, another major consideration with bonds is the credit risk, which boils down to the probability that the issuer will make the interest payments on time and redeem the bond at the maturity date. Treasurys, my favorite, are considered riskless. So they're not even rated at AAA, AAAA, or anything else. Consequently, all others—corporate and municipal bonds, mortgage-backed securities, emerging market debt, and so on—sell at higher yields than comparable Treasury maturities to account for higher risks. The higher the risk, the greater the spread, as was shown in March 2005 when GM announced big earnings troubles and investors pushed GM debt yields deep into junk bond territory.

As a result, the spreads between Treasurys and junk bonds and emerging market debt (see Figure 4.10) and even the spreads of investment-grade corporates (see Figure 4.11) leaped. Those spreads had narrowed earlier to ridiculously tiny levels due to the decline in defaults in recent years (see Figure 4.12) and the steep yield curve (see Figure 4.13), which encouraged the borrowing of cheap short-term money to finance the purchases of these bonds. But the Fed-led

FIGURE 4.10

Bond Yield Spreads

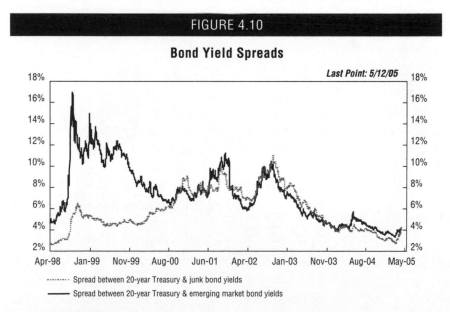

Last Point: 5/12/05

------- Spread between 20-year Treasury & junk bond yields
——— Spread between 20-year Treasury & emerging market bond yields

Source: Bianco Research

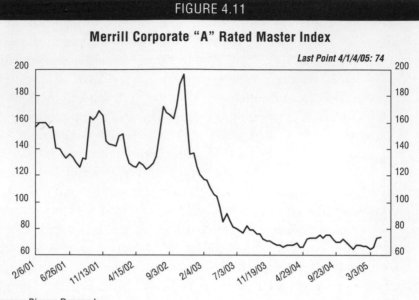

FIGURE 4.11

Merrill Corporate "A" Rated Master Index

Last Point 4/1/4/05: 74

Source: Bianco Research

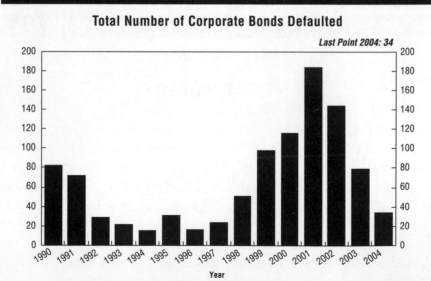

FIGURE 4.12

Total Number of Corporate Bonds Defaulted

Last Point 2004: 34

Source: Moody's Investors Services, Inc. and/or its affiliates. Reprinted with permission. All rights reserved.

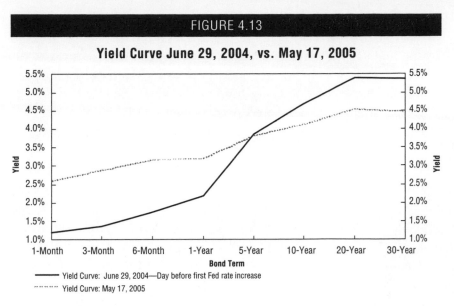

FIGURE 4.13

Yield Curve June 29, 2004, vs. May 17, 2005

Yield Curve: June 29, 2004—Day before first Fed rate increase
Yield Curve: May 17, 2005

Source: Federal Reserve and Ryan Labs, Inc.

rise in short rates since the central bank commenced tightening in June 2004, in combination with the decline in Treasury bond yields, squeezed out much of this carry trade money. And the GM bombshell announcement reversed the trend toward improving bond quality.

RISK AND MATURITY

Many seem to believe that bonds are for widows and orphans. They don't understand the volatility in bond prices that results from fluctuating interest rates and changes in credit quality. They clearly aren't aware of the leverage available to bond investors that can mean huge losses or, happily for me in our investments, substantial profits.

Some think that Treasurys are especially dull. They're oblivious to their three sterling qualities—they are the most riskless instruments in the world, they are the most liquid, and, unlike many corporate and municipal bonds, Treasurys usually can't be called before maturity. Otherwise, if interest rates are dropping, the issuers can refund their obligations and cut short the appreciation the bondholder receives.

And by the way, my interest in Treasurys or any other bonds is appreciation, not the coupon interest return. That's why I'm not attracted by the higher yield on corporates. Anyway, the spreads between corporates and Treasurys have been low for years, even before they fell further to those unrealistically low levels that definitely did not account for their risk, as I noted earlier. That fact became obvious to everyone, however, when those spreads leaped after the GM debacle.

Bond maturity is another hang-up for many individual investors. I saw this clearly years ago when we took over the management of my parents' investment accounts. It wasn't that they really trusted me, but their stockbroker of some twenty years retired, so a change was necessary. In any event, shortly thereafter my mother called and said, "Gary, I see that you put some Treasury bonds in our account that won't mature for thirty years." "That's right, Mom." "But Gary," she shot back, "Dad and I won't be alive in thirty years." I tried to explain that I didn't expect to hold them to maturity, but that, regardless, the longer the maturity, the greater the appreciation for a given decline in yields. I even went on to point out that stocks have no maturity, in effect, infinity, but 95-year-old people own them. I'm not sure my explanation completely or even partially convinced her.

THE COMPLEXITY OF STOCKS

After you consider the credit and interest rate risks and maturity considerations, there aren't a lot of other major issues for bondholders to worry about except perhaps the trend of inflation and Federal Reserve policy. But stocks have myriad factors that affect their total return. Think about the relationships of stock prices to earnings, to cash flow, and to book value, as well as dividend yields and payout ratios (see Figures 4.14 to 4.17).

Then there are all the difficult-to-quantify aspects such as the quality of a corporation's management and accounting, the regulatory atmosphere, the prospects for that industry, new product introductions, competition and product pricing, the general business climate, the health of the overall stock market, investor taste for risk, and so on. Anyone who believes that bonds, particularly Treasurys,

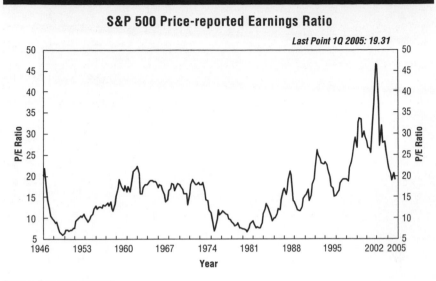

FIGURE 4.14

S&P 500 Price-reported Earnings Ratio

Last Point 1Q 2005: 19.31

Source: Standard & Poor's

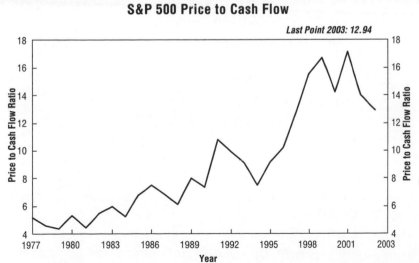

FIGURE 4.15

S&P 500 Price to Cash Flow

Last Point 2003: 12.94

Source: Haver Analytics

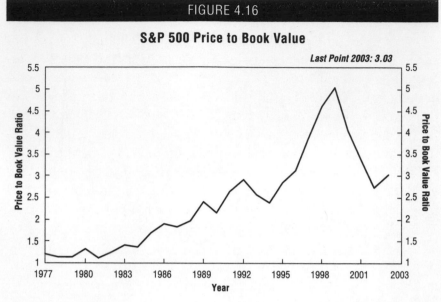

FIGURE 4.16

S&P 500 Price to Book Value

Last Point 2003: 3.03

Source: Haver Analytics

FIGURE 4.17

S&P 500 Dividends

Last Point: 1Q 2005

Payout ratio
Dividend yield

Source: Standard & Poor's

are complicated while stocks are simple to understand obviously lives in a different world than do I.

Why, then, are individual investors overwhelmingly devoted to stocks while showing scant attention to bonds? And note that reflecting investor interest, the financial TV news shows are almost entirely stock-oriented. This is driven home on CNBC by the indices displayed in the lower right-hand corner box on the TV screen. It flashes the levels of the Dow Industrials, the S&P 500, and the Nasdaq Composite Index *and* the changes, up or down, for the day.

But Treasurys, usually the ten-year note, only show the current yield. As a Treasury investor, I want to know the price change. That tells me if I am making or losing money in my positions that day. The current yield is much less interesting, and doesn't give any clue as to the price change unless I can remember the closing yield the previous day and know what each basis point change in yield means for the price change. Bloomberg, however, does show the changes in the Treasury note yield and price.

Furthermore, the investment emphasis on stocks is so widespread that many don't really think about other possibilities. When someone asks me, "How did the market do today?" I know he's referring to stocks, although I'm tempted to reply, "Which one? Stocks, bonds, crude oil, currencies, agricultural commodities, base metals, gold, or real estate?"

COCKTAIL PARTY PRATTLE

My guess is that investor zeal for stocks and not bonds stems from an innate human desire for risk, volatility and action. It isn't simply the desire to make big money quickly. Still, the same is true for bonds. You can buy Treasurys with 5 percent margin, and if that doesn't provide enough financial leverage and the opportunity for huge profits (or losses), there are always even more leveraged futures contracts.

The zeal for equities is also probably sparked by the desire to identify with an individual company and its products. For example, if an investor likes to drink Pepsi, he or she may well identify with that company and its stock. More important, success with an individual stock, especially an obscure one, gives the investor immense bragging opportunities at cocktail parties and other social gatherings.

I've personally tested this theory. In early 2005, when crude oil prices and energy stocks were soaring, I mentioned to several people at a cocktail party that we'd done very well with Suncor, which extracts oil from the tar sands in Canada. The resulting conversation was lively and the accolades for my investment prowess generous.

Then, with several other folks, I noted that we'd had a great day with Treasurys because our 30-year bonds had rallied one point. But by the time I explained that one point is only about 1 percent, but that our profits were huge since we use Treasury bond futures as well as zero-coupon bonds that give about twice the appreciation for a given decline in interest rates as coupon-paying bonds, the eyes of my listeners had glazed over or they were headed to the bar for another drink.

Individual investors also probably favor stocks over bonds because, like most Americans, they are optimistic by nature. And optimists look for rapid growth in economic activity and corporate profits, to the benefit of long stock positions. At the same time, they tend to associate bonds, especially Treasurys, with negative events. They regard them as safe havens during stock market collapses, recessions, and other bad times.

In addition, the bull market in stocks that ran from July 1982 to March 2000—17 years and 8 months (see Figure 4.6)—was so long and strong that it convinced many investors that stocks are the only long-term investment and will furnish attractive annual returns forever. Interestingly, this attitude has become so deeply ingrained that it survived the collapse in stocks in the early 2000s (see Figure 4.18).

THE PROS DON'T LIKE BONDS

Professional bond investors and those who underwrite them also, ironically, often seem to be negative on their own products. In the 1970s, I was the chief economist at White, Weld, an investment banking firm. The corporate finance people loved to take me along

FIGURE 4.18

Nasdaq Composite Index from January 1990 to May 2005

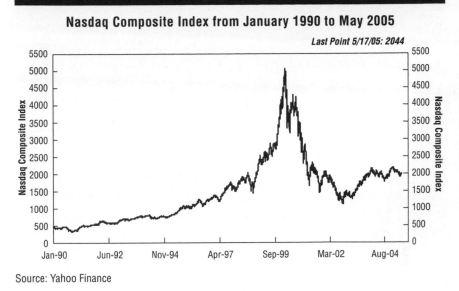

Last Point 5/17/05: 2044

Source: Yahoo Finance

on calls to bond underwriting prospects to discuss my economic outlook—but only if I was forecasting higher yields on bonds. A forecast of lower yields would encourage the prospect to delay issuing new bonds, but higher yields ahead spurred them to come to market soon and before their interest costs rose. My colleagues, of course, wanted the deals done immediately. A delayed underwriting might never get done, and even if it did, the fees would not be paid to White, Weld until later.

Professional managers of bond portfolios are also seldom optimistic over bond prices. As shown in Figure 4.9, they have been bearish for three years despite the considerable rally in bond prices in that time. Maybe the bond pros still recall vividly the high inflation days of the 1970s (refer back to Figure 4.1). Rising inflation rates propelled bond yields (Figure 4.5), so bondholders suffered as the prices of existing obligations fell. Adding to these losses, real bond yields were negative in the mid- and late 1970s (see Figure 4.19) as inflation spikes outran nominal yields. So they suffered a double whammy: First, portfolios fell in value, and second, current yields didn't even offset inflation.

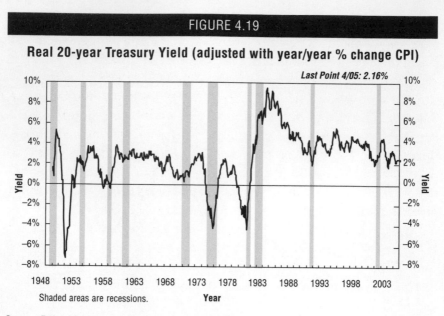

FIGURE 4.19

Real 20-year Treasury Yield (adjusted with year/year % change CPI)

Last Point 4/05: 2.16%

Shaded areas are recessions.

Source: Federal Reserve and Bureau of Labor Statistics

After those two disasters, bond investors refused to come back for thirds, and demanded—and got—very high yields in the early 1980s, as shown in Figure 4.19. Real yields have subsequently fallen back, but those earlier wrenching experiences may still linger in the minds of bond managers.

THE TEST OF HISTORY

Despite the overwhelming favoritism for stocks and disinterest, at least, for bonds by individual and professional investors alike, bonds have been far better investments in the last two decades, as least in the form we've used in many of our portfolios. Zero-coupon bonds do not pay the semi-annual interest that is normal with coupon bonds, but are issued at a discount to their redemption price. The interest earnings are reflected in the difference between the issue and redemption prices. With this configuration, the interest return is fixed, and there is no problem of reinvesting interest payments at lower and lower yields when market interest rates fall. So, zero-coupon bonds appreciate about twice as much for a given decline in interest rates as coupon bonds, as noted earlier. Unfortunately, it's symmetrical. The zero-coupon bond loses about twice as much if interest rates rise.

In October 1981, Treasury bond yields peaked at 14.7 percent. Suppose an investor bought a 25-year maturity, zero-coupon Treasury then and rolled it into another 25-year maturity in each subsequent year. Maintaining that maturity is important because the 25-year bond issued in 1981 now has less than two years to maturity, and the shorter the maturity, the smaller the price rise for a given decline in interest rates, as I mentioned earlier.

If that procedure had been followed, $100 invested in October 1981 would be worth $9,253 in April 2005, a 21.8 percent compound annual return. In contrast, $100 invested in the S&P 500 index at its bottom in July 1982 was worth $2,227 in April 2005, including reinvested dividends, or an 18.1 percent annual rate of gain. So, stocks did well, but even during their longest and strongest rally on record, the 25-year zero-coupon Treasury bonds did 4.2 times better (see Figure 4.20).

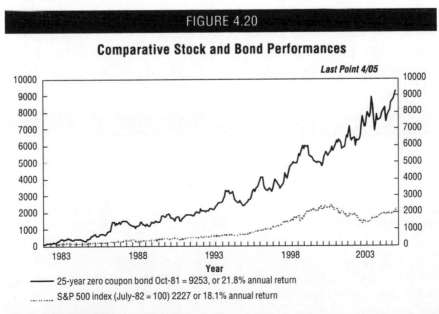

FIGURE 4.20

Comparative Stock and Bond Performances

Last Point 4/05

—— 25-year zero coupon bond Oct-81 = 9253, or 21.8% annual return

········· S&P 500 index (July-82 = 100) 2227 or 18.1% annual return

Source: Bianco Research

WHERE DO BONDS GO FROM HERE?

I believe that "the bond rally of a lifetime" that commenced in 1981 is still intact, and will take Treasury bond yields to a final low of 3.0 percent. This is the natural consequence of our forecast of mild deflation of 1 to 2 percent that is being promoted by powerful deflationary forces (see Table 4.2), the first seven of which are already hard at work. (See our two deflation books for full details, *Deflation: Why It's Coming, Whether It's Good or Bad, and How It Will Affect Your Investments, Business and Personal Affairs* (Lake View Publishing: 1998), and *Deflation: How to Survive and Thrive in the Coming Wave of Deflation* (McGraw-Hill: 1999)). After the 3.0 percent yields are reached, the big bonds appreciation will be over, but the 4 to 5 percent real returns on Treasury bonds will still be attractive compared to 2.5 percent in the post–World War II years to date (see Figure 4.19).

In this good deflation of excess supply, stocks will probably appreciate 1 to 2 percent and return 4 to 5 percent in total, assuming dividend yields return to what used to be their floor, 3 percent (see Figure 4.17). This means a total real stock return of 5 to 6 percent, in line with historical averages. The transition to good deflation, however, may be rough on the economy and on stocks, and for a few years may look like the bad deflation of deficient demand. This transition will entail substantial reductions in the current high levels of risks, financial leverage, and debt that are found

---

TABLE 4.2

Deflationary Forces

1. End of Cold War has reduced global defense spending.
2. Central banks still worry about inflation.
3. Restructuring persists globally.
4. The ongoing burst of new tech promotes productivity among producers and users of its gear.
5. Cost-cutting mass retailing is spreading worldwide.
6. Deregulation spurs competition.
7. Globalization will grow, fueling worldwide excess supply.
8. U.S. consumers will switch from borrowing and spending to saving.

Source: A. Gary Shilling & Co.

throughout financial markets and the economy, notably in the current housing bubble.

In any event, I'm sticking to the long-term investment theme that has served me well for almost 24 years—the unwinding of inflation and the resulting decline in Treasury bond yields. And I'm hoping that after more than two decades of unfolding, this theme remains distinctly nonconsensus. Only when the herd stampedes into my corral will I worry that "the bond rally of a lifetime" is ending.

CHAPTER 5

Risk Is Not a Knob

Ed Easterling, president of Crestmont Holdings, a Dallas-based investment and research firm, is the author of the book Unexpected Returns. *He also manages and advises on hedge fund portfolios. Ed is somewhat of an academic, serving on the adjunct faculty at the Cox School of Business at Southern Methodist University, where he teaches a course on hedge fund investment management for business school graduate students.*

Unexpected Returns *is one of the best easy-to-read books on stock market cycles. One of Ed's main focuses is the analysis and control of risk. If you're a serious investor, you'll find yourself returning to this chapter again and again.*   —John Mauldin

Risk Is Not a Knob

by Ed Easterling

⤳

"The first step toward making money is not losing it."

RISK CAN BE FRIEND OR FOE, AND AS AN INVESTOR YOU WILL SUCCEED OR FAIL depending on how you deal with it. Risk is an inherent condition of all investments and should be respected, assessed, managed, and prudently controlled. Your journey starts inside Wonderland, where "traditional" investment thinking operates. The journey continues through the looking glass into a state of reality.

You may have heard, "If you want greater returns, you have to take more risk." The implication is that risk creates returns—as though risk represents an element that mixes with investment capital to morph into returns. In reality, risk represents a condition that drives investors to demand compensation and protection. As a result, in the financial markets, higher returns tend to be associated with higher risks, which is far different than the notion that risk drives returns. By the end of this chapter, you will not view risk as fertilizer for your returns but rather as weeds in your investment garden. Your investment strategies will change to one that seeks higher returns and lower risk. This is important in all market environments, especially when market conditions reflect above-average valuations.

This chapter will explore return and risk and dispel the traditional view of risk and return. You will find ways to measure risk and examine why risk and volatility matter. As a result, you will identify ways to make better investment decisions.

RISKY BUSINESS

Risk is not an assumption based on historical averages; it is unique to each situation. Although risks can often be assessed in the context of history, the future does not necessarily mirror the past. A caution readily recognized (and often ignored!) appears in most investment documents: *"Past performance is not an indication of future results."* Likewise, past levels of risk do not necessarily indicate future risk.

Conventional wisdom about risk and long-term returns promotes a false sense of security based on the erroneous belief that interim losses yield future gains. Some investors assume that higher risk merely means near-term volatility rather than the possibility of permanent losses to their account.

Risk is uncertainty of a loss. Without uncertainty, the situation already would be a loss and not a risk. Further, without the possibility for loss—if the uncertainty is only about the size of your gain—there is hardly risk. Thus, despite all of the ways that risk can be measured and assessed, risk is the likelihood that your investment will lose money. It is often measured in terms of probability and magnitude. For example, an investment might have a 20 percent chance of a loss. Further, the investment could have a risk of losing 50 percent of the investment. As the probability of a loss increases and as the magnitude of potential loss increases, investments become more risky. The result is that investors should require greater potential for returns as risk increases.

Assessed together, returns and risk are elements that investors consider to determine the price and terms of an investment. If the assessment of return and risk is accurate, a properly structured portfolio of investments should deliver its expected return. Bear in mind, however, that on the other side of your transactions may be someone as diligent as you. As a buyer, you will believe that you have found great opportunity; the seller on the other side of your transaction believes that the opportunity was not worth the price. This capitalistic tension will be similar when you are the seller.

Therefore, be careful to use the diligence of a business decision to accurately assess the risks and potential returns.

MODERN PORTFOLIO MISUNDERSTANDINGS

Traditional portfolio logic holds that stocks are riskier than bonds since they have a greater potential for loss. An efficient market, as a result, will price stocks to deliver higher returns than bonds over the long term. Therefore, the logic goes, investors should increase their stock holdings in order to generate higher returns. For risk-averse investors, an efficient mix of stocks and bonds offers the best characteristics of return and risk.

The flaw in this argument is that market fundamentals can drive stocks to price levels that make it difficult to earn good returns in the future. The expected returns for highly priced stocks can be very low; they may even remain negative for years. In these circumstances, stocks are priced at levels that may provide a lower return than bonds. An investor who adopts the traditional logic that higher risk leads to higher returns and increases his stock allocation at a time of high stock valuations may be lowering his expected return rather than increasing it. The investor is simultaneously increasing his risk and lowering his expected return for years into the future.

Stocks are indeed riskier than bonds. History and the operation of rational markets have shown that stocks should return more than bonds over the long run, but the degree of risk in stocks varies greatly, depending on market valuations. Stocks are most risky when valuations, reflected in prices, are high. This is when the risks of decline and loss are greatest.

Higher risks can lead to higher losses unless addressed with the tools of risk management. To reiterate, *risk is not a knob to be turned for greater returns*. Turning the knob invites more risk; it does not drive returns. During the past few decades, modern portfolio theories became inverted as investors were led to believe that higher returns necessarily emanate from higher risk.

However, risk does not drive returns; returns are what investors seek to compensate for the effects of risk by appropriately pricing the investment.

RISK MISCONCEPTIONS

Rational investors generally require riskier investments to offer higher returns than less risky investments. This bedrock financial concept governs much investment thinking and is why lower-quality bonds yield more than higher-quality bonds. But the risk/reward relationship is not always as direct as many might assume. Did Jack Welch at GE or Warren Buffett take on higher levels of risk to achieve their higher-than-average levels of return? Most analysts would say that Welch and Buffett achieved higher returns by exercising higher levels of skill than their counterparts. Analysts might even argue that a portion of their success lies in their ability to reduce risk by identifying particularly high-quality companies to add to their investment and corporate portfolios. Some investment strategies employing an absolute-return approach have generated higher returns over market cycles while assuming demonstrably less risk than the overall market.

Another misconception is that higher risk automatically means a potential for higher rewards. Risk is what rational investors assess and price into the expected return of an investment. The reason lower-quality bonds have higher yields than higher-quality bonds is that investors demand more yield for the riskier bond. The price of the lower-quality bond is set by rational investors who would not pay a price that does not compensate for the risk. It is the function of the market to set the price and terms of assets or investments with the expected financial payback based on the anticipated level of risk and losses.

EXPECTED RETURNS AND PROBABLE RETURNS

The phrase *expected returns* is used in the financial community to refer to the rate of return that an investor should require from a certain investment, given its risk profile. In 1952, when Harry Markowitz published the principles of Modern Portfolio Theory in *The Journal of Finance*, he referred to the "expected returns—variance of returns" rule, where the expected returns "include an allowance for risk."

And so, expected returns, other than yields from risk-free Treasury bills, include a *risk premium*—a gross yield before any losses. In comparing higher- and lower-quality bonds, the lower-quality bond is priced to yield higher interest payments due its greater risks. Compare, for example, a higher-quality U.S. Treasury bond yielding 5 percent, with a lower-quality bond issued by a risky company. Due to the greater risk of loss, investors should require that the corporate bond have a higher yield, say 10 percent. Since there is generally no risk of loss on the Treasury bond, the expected return of 5 percent will be 5 percent. But the expected return of 10 percent on the corporate bond may be realized at 10 percent, or it may be less if there is a credit loss.

In a portfolio diversified across numerous corporate bonds yielding 10 percent, it should be expected that the realized portfolio return will be less than 10 percent. It is likely that at least a few losses will occur given the higher risk profile of the bonds. As a result, there will be a difference between *pre-risk expected yield* and *post-risk probable yield*. Investors are often seduced into higher-yielding investments without considering the likely post-risk return. It is important to understand this when considering the risk premium of asset classes, including stocks.

MEASURING RISK

There are many ways to assess and measure risk, including methods for quantifying the probability or magnitude of a loss. Investors use these measures to determine the likelihood of losing money on an investment and to estimate how much they could lose if the investment fails to perform as expected.

Risks can be categorized as general risks of an asset class or as risks associated with individual investment choices. For example, the risk of the stock market as a whole is different from the risks associated with individual securities. It is important to understand this difference in order to manage the risks and the source of your returns.

ABSOLUTE PROBABILITIES

Probabilities are only true if they are statistically valid. Without a preponderance of evidence, a probability is little more than an educated guess. For example, one investment with a 10 percent probability of a total loss will result in either a total success or a total loss. A 10 percent probability of total loss over 100 transactions, however, usually results in losses of close to 10 percent across the portfolio. Unless your portfolio is sufficiently diversified, most measures of risk will not accurately assess the threat to your portfolio.

Let's say you have the opportunity to invest in an oil well with a 25 percent probability of success and a payoff of ten times your investment. Your expected return would be 250 percent. If, on the one hand, you invest $12,000 across a portfolio of a dozen ventures, you can expect to lose $9,000 with nine of them but make $30,000 from the three in which you invested $3,000. Your net return of $30,000 represents a 250 percent return on your $12,000.

On the other hand, if you invest all $12,000 in one project, the probabilities and expected return are the same, but the outcome will be binary—it will either succeed or fail. If you succeed, your return is 1,000 percent and if you fail, your loss is 100 percent. The statistical probabilities may be the same, but the risk and return profiles are quite different. This is one of the benefits and strengths of diversification.

SHORT-TERM AND LONG-TERM

For the stock you buy today, risk can be regarded as the probability and magnitude of a loss tomorrow, or whenever you sell it. Some believe a "loss is not a loss until you take it." As a result, many assess risk against the absolute level of break-even. In the short run, over days or even a few years, break-even can be a close proxy against which to assess risk. In the longer run, however, risk takes on additional meanings.

Figure 5.1 reflects the total net return after transaction costs for the S&P 500 Index over every ten-year period since 1900. There have been ninety-five such ten-year periods starting with 1900–1909, followed by 1901–1910, and ending with 1995–2004. Market pundits will comfort you with the statistic that over ten-year periods investors have lost money only three times since 1900 and never since 1941. Therefore, they contend, there is little risk to stock market investments over the long term.

Their contention ignores two significant issues that become much more relevant over longer periods of time: inflation and liabilities.

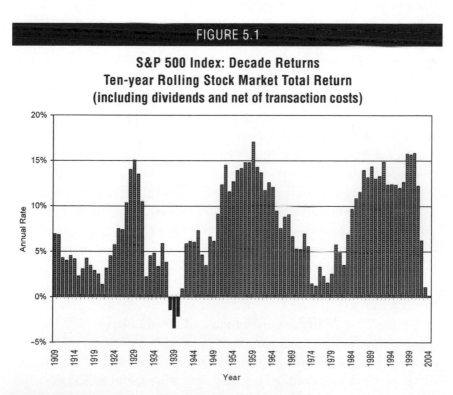

FIGURE 5.1

S&P 500 Index: Decade Returns
Ten-year Rolling Stock Market Total Return
(including dividends and net of transaction costs)

Since money represents purchasing power, an investment that breaks even over a decade returns only a fraction of the purchasing power, after inflation, that it had when it was initially deployed for an expected return. Over short periods, the effects are minimal, but over longer periods of time the effect of inflation compounds. In the course of a decade, that which costs $1 will cost $1.41, given the historical average inflation rate of 3.5 percent. If your investment breaks even over that period, you will be almost 30 percent short of meeting your obligations. In some instances, obligations rise at a higher rate than inflation. This can apply to institutions as well as to individuals.

Institutions, including pension plans and endowments, have liabilities they are required to fund with returns from their investment portfolio. Individuals have retirement goals or family responsibilities that demand an expected rate of return. If the investment return over a decade or two is break-even for an institution or an individual, risk of loss has not been avoided; rather, risk has been experienced as the loss of the required return. Although the investment may not have lost money, the institution or individual could be bankrupt as increasing liabilities outstrip break-even or small-return assets.

For example, if a pension plan has $100 million in assets and is required to fund $200 million in liabilities in ten years, it will need to earn 7.2 percent a year. Likewise, if an individual has a ten-year retirement plan or education goal and expects a certain return, simply breaking even can be disappointing or even disastrous.

For the purpose of assessing portfolio risk, it is clear that a measure and assessment other than break-even is necessary. Rather than simply recovering the principal, investors should assess the probability of achieving the required or expected rate of return. Risk, therefore, represents the uncertainty of a shortfall in achieving the projected liability.

Figure 5.2 recognizes the demands of institutional and individual future obligations and assesses the performance of the stock market over the past century for its ability to meet these obligations. Figure 5.2 is identical to the chart in Figure 5.1 with a line reflecting a required net return of 7 percent. The net return includes commissions,

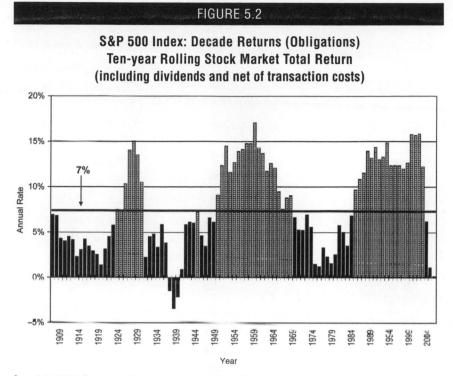

FIGURE 5.2

S&P 500 Index: Decade Returns (Obligations)
Ten-year Rolling Stock Market Total Return
(including dividends and net of transaction costs)

bid/ask spreads, investment management fees, execution slippage, and other transaction costs of 2 percent annually in the aggregate. Figure 5.2 reveals the historical probability of achieving success without risking funding shortfalls for obligations or planned uses.

Over the ninety-five decade-long periods since 1900, only forty-five have achieved annual returns of 7 percent or more—a 47 percent probability of success!

Further, of the forty-five periods that do reflect sufficient returns, thirty-seven (82 percent) are periods with price/earnings (P/E) ratios that increased from the start of the period to the end of the period. To rationally include an assumption of 7 percent net returns for a stock-market portfolio, history suggests that rising P/E ratios are virtually required. To assume otherwise is to ignore risk and rely on hope.

VOLATILITY GREMLINS

Beyond probabilities and actual losses, many market experts measure risk by volatility of the returns. The most common measure is *standard deviation*, a statistic that reflects the width of the range for returns. A low value indicates that returns are expected to be in a narrow range, while a higher value indicates that the returns are more dispersed.

This matters over time because volatility diminishes compounded returns compared to average returns. The quality of the ride also makes a difference. Sharp downdrafts and roller-coaster volatility can drive many investors to divest their stock holdings. As a result, investors would experience the decline but not the recovery. Further, significant volatility can leave an investor vulnerable to his need for capital just when it would be required to enjoy the investment benefits of an upward swing.

Investors cannot spend the average returns that are often cited to promote stocks as consistently good investments. Investors can only spend compounded returns. The distinction between the two is important; an example will highlight the differences.

A simple return is the mathematical average of a set of numbers. For example, the simple average of 10 percent and 20 percent is 15 percent. A compounded return is the single annual percentage that provides the cumulative effect of a series of returns. If an investment grew by 10 percent and then again by 20 percent, its cumulative increase would be 32 percent. This is greater than the sum of 10 percent and 20 percent as a result of compounding. However, the single percentage that would grow to 32 percent over two periods is 14.9 percent, slightly less than the simple average of 15 percent.

In Figure 5.3, the simple average of the annual changes for the stock market was 7.3 percent during the period from 1900–2004. The compounded annual change, reflecting a more accurate view of realized annual returns, was only 5 percent for the same period. Although total returns were slightly higher, since dividends generally were greater than transaction costs over that period, the difference between simple returns and compounded returns is dramatic.

FIGURE 5.3

Volatility Gremlins: Effect on Compounded Returns

Simple Annual Changes

	'00	'01	'02	'03	'04	'05	'06	'07	'08	'09	Average
1900	7%	−9%	0%	−24%	42%	38%	−2%	−38%	47%	15%	
1910	−18%	0%	8%	−10%	−31%	82%	−4%	−22%	11%	30%	
1920	−33%	13%	22%	−3%	26%	30%	0%	29%	48%	−17%	
1930	−34%	−53%	−23%	67%	4%	39%	25%	−33%	28%	−3%	
1940	−13%	−15%	8%	14%	12%	27%	−8%	2%	−2%	13%	
1950	18%	14%	8%	−4%	44%	21%	2%	−13%	34%	16%	Avg. = 7.3%
1960	−9%	19%	−11%	17%	15%	11%	−19%	15%	4%	−15%	
1970	5%	6%	15%	−17%	−28%	38%	18%	−17%	−3%	4%	
1980	15%	−9%	20%	20%	−4%	28%	23%	2%	12%	27%	
1990	−4%	20%	4%	14%	2%	33%	26%	23%	16%	25%	
2000	−6%	−7%	−17%	25%	3%						

Compounded Annual Change | | | | Average

	Jan 1	Dec 31	
	1900	2004	
Start	66		
End		10,783	Avg. = 5.0%
Years		105	

Excluding dividends, transaction costs, and taxes, the simple average change of 7.3 percent provides the illusion that had you invested $1,000 in the market in 1900, you would have $1,632,942 by the end of 2004 ($1,000 compounded at 7.3 percent annually over 105 years yields $1,632,942). An investor in the stock market over that same period, however, would net $167,833 because the compounded effect on returns was only 5 percent annually over the 105 years. The average return is quite different from the compounded return. Compounded returns are the relevant returns that generate cash in your account that can be spent.

Although the average return was 7.3 percent, if your investments are only compounding at 5 percent, the financial results will be significantly lower. The difference between the average return and the compounded return is the result of two effects called *volatility gremlins*. These volatility gremlins can reduce the dollars you actually receive by almost 90 percent!

The volatility gremlins erode the average return into the compounded return and the simple return into the actual return. Negative numbers and the dispersion of returns around the average are mathematical mites. Each has a significant effect on realized returns.

By understanding their impact, investors can appreciate the benefits of reducing volatility and increasing the consistency of investment returns. Investors can then realize higher compounded returns and experience a more enjoyable and less stressful investment ride.

The first volatility gremlin is the impact of negative numbers on compounded returns. To illustrate the effect, consider an investment over two years. Make 20 percent the first year and lose 20 percent the second year. The simple average return is zero, for when +20 percent is added to –20 percent, the sum is 0 percent. When 0 percent is divided by the number of years (two, in our example), the simple average return is 0 percent. Yet, an investor will actually lose 4 percent. To break even, it takes a greater positive return than the offsetting negative loss. For –20 percent, the offset is +25 percent. It works the same, whether the positive or the negative occurs first.

The second volatility gremlin is the impact of the range of returns on the average. As the returns in a series become more dispersed from the average, the compounded return declines. This second dynamic is demonstrated in the following example. The compounded return from three periods of 5 percent returns is greater than any other sequence that averages 5 percent. Figure 5.4 illustrates this mathematical phenomenon. If you earn a return of 5 percent per year for three years in a row, your simple average return is 5 percent, and your compounded return is 5 percent. If, however, you earn 6 percent the first year, 5 percent the second year, and 4 percent the third year, your simple average return remains 5 percent, but your compounded return drops to 4.997 percent. Although this minor difference appears insignificant, let's consider the ramifications.

The greater the volatility of the returns, the greater the drop in the compounded return. Consider a case in which you earn 9 percent the first year, 5 percent the second year, and 1 percent the third year. Your simple average return remains 5 percent, but your compounded rate of return—the return that gives you dollars to spend—drops to 4.949 percent. The actual volatility of the stock market is greater still, and the impact on compounded returns is much more significant. Keep in mind that half of all years in the

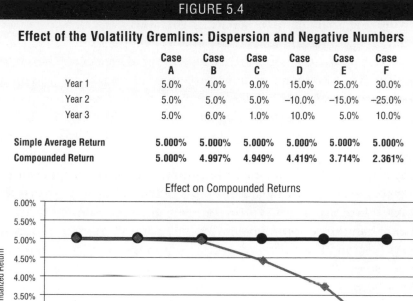

FIGURE 5.4

Effect of the Volatility Gremlins: Dispersion and Negative Numbers

	Case A	Case B	Case C	Case D	Case E	Case F
Year 1	5.0%	4.0%	9.0%	15.0%	25.0%	30.0%
Year 2	5.0%	5.0%	5.0%	−10.0%	−15.0%	−25.0%
Year 3	5.0%	6.0%	1.0%	10.0%	5.0%	10.0%
Simple Average Return	**5.000%**	**5.000%**	**5.000%**	**5.000%**	**5.000%**	**5.000%**
Compounded Return	**5.000%**	**4.997%**	**4.949%**	**4.419%**	**3.714%**	**2.361%**

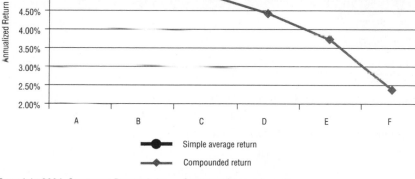

Effect on Compounded Returns

Legend:
— Simple average return
— Compounded return

stock market occur outside of a 32 percent range, from −16 percent to +16 percent. As the level of dispersion increases, the impact from the second volatility gremlin increases.

PORTFOLIO MANAGEMENT

If the first rule of portfolio management is diversification, why do most investors concentrate their risks? Many investors believe that a portfolio constructed with numerous stocks and bonds is diversified. That approach has its roots in the principles of *modern portfolio theory* (MPT). But when MPT is misapplied, it does not provide the road map to secure investing and leaves investors vulnerable to substantial risk.

A key principle of MPT, which was developed by Harry Markowitz in the early 1950s, is simple to understand yet striking in its implications: Diversification can eliminate the risks that do not provide returns while retaining the risks that do provide returns. William F. Sharpe further developed these principles into the capital asset pricing model (CAPM). Every investment carries two distinct risks. One is the risk of being in the market, which Sharpe called *systematic risk*. This risk, later dubbed *beta*, cannot be diversified away. The other, *unsystematic risk*, is specific to a company's fortunes. Since this uncertainty can be mitigated through appropriate diversification, Sharpe figured that a portfolio's expected return hinges solely on its beta—its relationship to the overall market. The CAPM helps measure portfolio risk and the return an investor can expect for taking that risk.

In combination, MPT and CAPM have been the means for structuring investment portfolios for the past several decades. Based on an investor's risk profile, allocations are made across investment alternatives. Decades ago, there were stocks and bonds, and occasionally an alternative investment. As a result, portfolios were developed from a very limited palette. MPT and CAPM were groundbreaking principles that helped investors and advisors structure diversified portfolios of stocks and bonds rather than concentrated portfolios.

As simple as this sounds—and those concepts are second nature in investing today—Dr. Sharpe determined that market risk is the only risk investors are paid to include in their portfolios. Since the risks associated with individual companies can be diversified away, the systematic market risk is the source of returns. Investors may have heard this put another way: "Eighty to 90 percent of returns come from being in the market, and a fraction comes from stock selection." Actually, if an investor is diversified in accord with theory, then CAPM indicates that the percentage of the returns that is due to the market should be 100 percent. As a result, effective diversification under MPT and CAPM should provide investors with investment returns that are consistent with market returns.

These principles can be applied both to stocks and bonds. A diversified portfolio of stocks tends to provide the returns of the stock market as a whole. Once individual company risk is diversified, the pure stock market risk remains. Thus, the portfolio moves with the stock market. Stock market returns are driven by earnings, growth, and valuation changes (as measured by the price/earnings ratio, or P/E). If P/E increases, stock market returns are generally high, since the P/E ratio multiplies the effect of rising earnings. If P/E ratios decrease, stock market returns will be low or negative, since declining P/Es generally offset the benefit of rising earnings.

For example, consider a stock that sells for $15 and has earnings per share of $1. The P/E ratio is fifteen ($15 divided by $1). If the earnings increase by 5 percent to $1.05 and the P/E ratio remains the same, the stock price will rise to $15.75, since the stock price equals the earnings per share multiplied by the P/E ratio. If, however, the P/E rises to twenty in addition to the increase in earnings to $1.05, the stock price will be $21.00, a gain of 40 percent over the initial price of $15.00. As a result, approximately one-eighth (5 percent) of the gain comes from the 5 percent growth in earnings, and the balance comes from the increase in the P/E ratio. However, if the P/E ratio declines to ten while earnings increase to $1.05, the stock price will be $10.50. Even though earnings grew by 5 percent, the investor will lose 30 percent on the investment. As you can see, the impact of changes in the P/E ratio can have a dramatic impact on the stock price and an investor's return.

With bonds, once the individual company risks are diversified, the portfolio moves in concert with the bond market, which is largely driven by trends in interest rates. As many investors have experienced, when interest rates decline, bond values increase. Likewise, rising interest rates cause bond values to decline. Thus, if interest rates are falling, the yield from the bond portfolio is supplemented with increases in the value of the bonds. If rates are rising, the decline in bond prices offsets some of the portfolio yield, resulting in lower total returns.

Therefore, an investment portfolio with allocations of 60 percent in a diversified stock portfolio, 30 percent in a diversified bond portfolio, and 10 percent in other investments, has a 90 percent concentration across two risks: stock market risk and bond market risk. Over time, these two markets tend to move in the same direction and essentially represent a similar risk to the investor.

This does not indicate that MPT and CAPM are not solid principles, but that the application of the principles has not evolved along with the increasingly complex financial markets. Dr. Markowitz's 1952 publication of MPT discussed the concept of "performances of available securities." In 1952, stocks and bonds were the predominant investment vehicles. A portfolio allocated across the two asset classes was about as diversified as you could get.

Mutual funds were uncommon before the 1980s: There were fewer than 300 in the 1960s but more than 10,000 today. Moreover, investment choices and available securities have exploded over the past two decades. Today, there are asset-backed securities, foreign exchanges, real estate, options, a variety of commodities, investment trusts, hedge funds, inflation-protected bonds, and so on.

Most investors remember only the market risks and conditions of the past two decades, when annual trends strongly supported stock and bond investors. Interim dips were always buying opportunities. Investors with battle scars from the 1970s and earlier, however, know that stock and bond market risks are not always so forgiving. The driver of stocks—the P/E ratio—is again at historic highs. The driver of bonds—interest rates—is near recent historic lows. Given the position of the traditional asset classes, the odds appear to favor Mr. Risk over Mr. Return for stocks and bonds.

The financial community has also realized that Eugene Fama's *efficient market hypothesis* (EMH), an important assumption for MPT and CAPM, may not be as strict as originally theorized. Financial markets are a process rather than a condition. In other words, while markets attempt to find the right prices over time, they do not possess all the information all the time. Many alternative investments today—hedge funds, for example—profit from mispricings and inefficiencies, and in doing so contribute to the efficiency of the markets.

Returning to Dr. Markowitz, diversification in a portfolio applies to risks, not securities. Other than not being familiar with investment alternatives, what else might explain why investors concentrate their portfolios in two similar risks when so many options are available?

FRONT STAGE: YOUR ASSUMPTIONS

The *relative return investment philosophy* is largely based on three theories: Harry Markowitz's modern portfolio theory (MPT), Eugene Fama's efficient market hypothesis (EMH), and William Sharpe's capital asset pricing model (CAPM). Stated simply, MPT explains how risk-averse investors can construct portfolios to optimize expected returns based upon a given level of market risk. EMH posits that the price of securities reflects all known information and inhibits investors from choosing mispriced securities. CAPM provides a framework for constructing portfolios with an optimal reward and risk relationship.

MPT, EMH, and CAPM profoundly influence the thinking of many of the world's largest institutional investors, and rightly so. They provide valuable insights into risk, market efficiency, investment theory, and portfolio construction. MPT and CAPM most directly affect investment management and portfolio construction. They rely on key assumptions regarding rational investors and efficient markets. They also rely on the user to determine appropriate assumptions for future returns. As Dr. Markowitz stated in his 1952 article, "Portfolio Theory" in *The Journal of Finance:*

> The process of selecting a portfolio may be divided into two stages. The first stage starts with observation and experience and ends with beliefs about the future performances of available securities. The second stage starts with the relevant beliefs about future performances and ends with the choice of the portfolio.

Dr. Markowitz emphasized that MPT relies on the user to identify the available securities and develop assumptions about their future performances. If market conditions value an asset class at a relatively high level, and it is therefore expected to perform below average for a period of time, MPT requires that its assumptions include below-average returns for that asset class. If average returns are assumed, the results from MPT will be skewed. Estimating future returns is always a challenge, but too many investors rely on average historical returns rather than base likely future returns on existing valuations. Particularly when the environment is biased in the direction of below-average returns, investors often underestimate the level of risk in their portfolios.

IN CONCLUSION: CAVEAT INVESTOR

Determine the risks inherent in potential investments, assess the reward potential, and make rational and prudent decisions. Shy away from unacceptable risks, and position your portfolio to profit consistently.

Whether you take the traditional approach of relative return investing or the progressive approach of skill-based investing, risk is integral in your portfolio. Savvy investors understand the risks and their underlying assumptions and adopt a more businesslike approach to investing, reducing or hedging unwanted or undesirable risks.

Investors are too often surprised by losses from unexpected or unintended risks. A well-constructed investment portfolio, like a well-run business, addresses its vulnerabilities and reacts to the ever-changing environment.

Risk, when it becomes a loss, undermines the value of previous or future gains. The power of losses exceeds the power of gains, requiring ever-greater gains to restore increasing losses. As risk and the variability of returns increase, the force of Albert Einstein's eighth wonder of the world—compound interest—is diminished.

Beware the pundit who cheers an investment for not losing money over the long term. The effects of inflation and potentially rising financial obligations require that success be measured by the achievement of solid returns. There is much risk in simply breaking even in the long run.

Most important, remember the first principle of Markowitz's Nobel Prize-winning modern portfolio theory: Assumptions are your responsibility. Be sure that your assumptions reasonably and rationally assess risk as you develop, structure, and diversify your investment portfolio. Keep in mind that the long-term average is rarely a good assumption.

Risk is an ingredient in every investment, not simply a key to higher returns.

CHAPTER 6

Psychology Matters: An Investors' Guide to Thinking about Thinking

James Montier is the global equity strategist for Dresdner, Kleinwort Wasserstein based in London, England. He is the author of Behavioural Finance—Insights Into Irrational Minds and Markets. *At age 33, he has already produced a significant body of work analyzing numerous books, studies, and research papers on the neurological and psychological reasons for our investment decision-making process.*

James is an economist by training who has worked in financial markets for the last ten years. James spent time in Japan and Hong Kong, a great stomping ground for bear market training. He has also taught behavioral finance at a U.K. university. —John Mauldin

Psychology Matters: An Investors' Guide to Thinking about Thinking

by James Montier

∽

INVESTING IS ALL ABOUT MAKING CHOICES AND DECISIONS. YET MANY IN-vestors give little or no thought as to how they actually go about making decisions. Imagine that you receive a new oven. Would you unpack it, plug it in, and try and cook something? (Obviously if you are male the answer is yes, falling back on the instruction manual only when all else fails!). Of course, the prudent answer would be no. Having an oven and being able to cook are two very different things. However, we assume that simply because we have a brain, we all know how to use it perfectly.

What goes on inside our heads when we make decisions? Un-derstanding how our brains work is vital to understanding the deci-sions we take. One of the most exciting developments in cognitive psychology over recent years has been the development of dual process theories of thought. I know that sounds dreadful, but it isn't. It is really a way of saying that we tend to have two different ways of thinking embedded in our minds.

ARE YOU SPOCK OR McCOY?

For the Trekkies out there, these two systems can, perhaps, be characterized as Dr. McCoy and Mr. Spock. In the TV series *Star Trek*, McCoy was irrepressibly human, forever allowing his emo-tions to rule the day. In contrast, Spock (half human, half Vulcan) was determined to suppress his emotions, letting logic drive his decisions.

McCoy's approach would seem to be founded in system X. System X is essentially the emotional part of the brain. It is automatic and effortless in the way that it processes information. That is to say, the X-system prescreens information before we are consciously aware that it even made an impact on our minds. Hence, X-system is effectively the default option. X-system deals with information in an associative way. Its judgments tend to be based on similarity (of appearance) and closeness in time. Because of the way X-system deals with information, it can handle vast amounts of data simultaneously. To computer geeks, it is a rapid parallel processing unit. For the X-system to believe that something is valid it may simply need to wish that it were so.

System C is the "Vulcan" part of the brain. To use it requires deliberate effort. It is logical and deductive in the way in which it handles information. Because it is logical, it can only follow one step at a time. Hence, in computing terms it is a slow serial processing unit. In order to convince the C-system that something is true, logical argument and empirical evidence will be required. Table 6.1 provides a summary of the main differences between the two systems.

This dual system approach to the way the mind works has received support from very recent studies by neuroscientists. They have begun to attach certain parts of the brain to certain functions. In order to do this, neuroscientists ask experiment participants to perform tasks while their brains are being monitored via electroencephalograms (EEG), positron emission tomography (PET), or—most often of late—functional magnetic resonance imaging (fMRI). The outcomes are then compared to base cases and the differences between the scans highlight the areas of the brain that are being utilized.

Table 6.2 lays out some of the major neural correlates for the two systems of thinking that were previously outlined. There is one very important thing to note about these groupings: the X-system components are much older in terms of human development. They evolved a long time before the C-system correlates.

TABLE 6.1

Two Systems of Reasoning

System One: Experiential X-system/Reflexive/Intuitive	System Two: Rational C-system/Reflective
Holistic	Analytic
Affective (what feels good)	Logical
Associative—judgments based on similarity and temporal contiguity	Deductive
Rapid parallel processing	Slow, serial processing
Concrete images	Abstract images
Slower to change	Changes with speed of thought
Crudely differentiated—broad generalization	More highly differentiated
Crudely integrated—context-specific processing	More high integrated—cross-context processing
Experienced passively and preconsciously	Experienced actively and consciously
Automatic and effortless	Controlled and effortful
Self-evidently valid: "Experiencing is believing," or perhaps wishing is believing	Requires justification via logic and evidence

Source: Modified from Epstein (1991)

TABLE 6.2

Neural Correlates of the Two Reasoning Systems

X-system	C-system
Amygdala	Anterior cingulate cortex
Basal ganglia	Prefrontal cortex
Lateral temporal cortex	Medial temporal lobe

Source: DrKW Macro Research

THE PRIMACY OF EMOTION

This evolutionary age edge helps to explain why the X-system is the default option for information processing. We needed emotions far before we needed logic. This is perhaps best explained by an example using fear. As explained by Joseph LeDoux, fear is one of the better-understood emotions.[1] Fear seems to be served by two neural pathways. One is fast and dirty (LeDoux's low road), the other more reflective and logical (the high road). The links to the two systems of thinking should be obvious.

Imagine standing in front of a glass container with a snake inside. The snake rears up, the danger is perceived, and the sensory thalamus processes the information. From here, two signals emerge. On the low road, the signal is sent to the amygdala, part of the X-system (also known as the *limbic system*), and the brain's center for fear and risk. The amygdala reacts fast, and forces you to jump back.

However, the second signal (taking the high road) sends the information to the sensory cortex, which in a more conscious fashion assesses the possible threat. This is the system that points out that there is a layer of glass between you and the snake. However, from a survival viewpoint, a false positive is a far better response than a false negative!

EMOTIONS: BODY OR BRAIN?

Most people tend to think that emotions are the conscious response to events or actions. That is, something happens and your brain works out the emotional response—be it sadness, anger, happiness, or some other emotion. Then your brain tells your body how to react—for example, tear up, pump blood, or increase the breathing rate.

William James, the grandfather of modern psychology, was among the first to posit that true causality may well flow from the body to the brain. In James's view of the world, the brain assesses the situation so quickly that there simply isn't time for us to become consciously aware of how we should feel. Instead, the brain surveys the body, takes the results (i.e., skin sweating, increased heartbeat), and then infers the emotion that matches physical signals that the body has generated.

If you want to try this yourself, try creating the face that matches the emotion you wish to experience. For instance, try smiling. If you sit with a smile on your face, concentrating on that smile, soon enough you are likely to start to feel the positive emotions that one associates with smiling.[2]

An entertaining example of the body's impact on decisions is provided by Epley and Gilovich (2001).[3] They asked people to evaluate headphones. While conducting the evaluation, participants were asked to either nod or shake their heads. Those who were asked to nod their heads during the evaluation gave much more favorable ratings than those asked to shake their heads.

In the words of Gilbert and Gill,[4] we are *momentary realists*. That is to say, we have a tendency to trust our initial emotional reaction and correct that initial view "only subsequently, occasionally and effortfully." For instance, when we stub a toe on a rock or bang our head on a beam (an easy thing to do in my house), we curse the inanimate object despite the fact it could not possibly have done anything to avoid our own mistake.

EMOTION: GOOD, BAD, OR BOTH?

However, emotion may be needed in order to allow us to actually make decisions. There are a group of people who, through tragic accidents or radical surgery, have had the emotional areas of their minds damaged. These individuals did not become the walking optimizers known as *homo economicus*. Rather, in many cases, these individuals are now actually incapable of making decisions. They make endless plans but never get around to implementing any of them.[5]

Bechara et al.[6] devised an experiment to show how the lack of emotion in such individuals can lead them to make suboptimal decisions. They played a gambling game with both controls (players without damage to the emotional centers of the brain) and patients (those with damage to the emotional parts of the brain). Each player was sat in front of four packs of cards (A, B, C, and D). Players were given a loan of $2,000 and told that the object of the games was to avoid losing the loan, while trying to make as much extra money as possible. They were also told that turning cards from each of the packs would generate gains and occasional losses. The players were told the impact of each card after each turn, but no running score was given.

Turning cards from packs A and B paid $100, while C and D paid only $50. Unpredictably, the turning of some cards carried a penalty, such that consistently playing packs A and B led to an overall loss. Playing from C and D led to an overall gain.

Performance was assessed at various stages of the game. Four different periods were identified. The first involved no loss in either pack (prepunishment); the second phase was when players reported they had no idea about the game, and no feeling about the packs. The third was found only in the controls, who started to say they had a hunch about packs A and B being riskier. Only in the last phase could the (conceptual) players articulate that A and B were riskier.

Table 6.3 shows the average number of rounds in each phase, and the percentage of players making it through each phase of the game. The patients without emotions were unable to form hunches, and far fewer survived the game.

Now cast your eyes over Figures 6.1 and 6.2. Figure 6.1 shows the number of cards drawn from packs A and B (bad) and C and D

TABLE 6.3

Progress over the Game

	Number of Rounds		Survivor Percentage	
	Controls	Patients	Controls	Patients
Prepunishment	0–10	0–10	100	100
Prehunch	10–50	9–80	100	100
Hunch	50–80		100	
Conceptual	80+	80+	70	50

Source: Bechara et al. (1997)

FIGURE 6.1

Average Number of Cards Drawn from Bad and Good Packs: The Controls

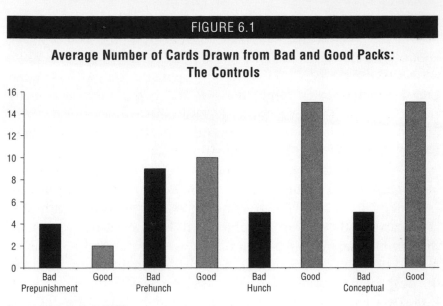

Source: Bechara et al. (1997)

FIGURE 6.2

Average Number of Cards Drawn from Bad and Good Packs: The Patients

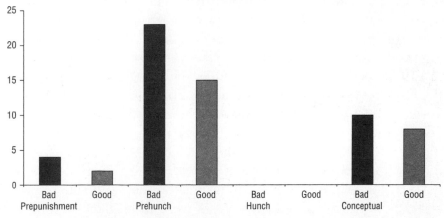

Source: Bechara et al. (1997)

(good) in each phase by the controls. In the prehunch phase, they are already favoring the good packs marginally. In the hunch phase, controls are clearly favoring the good packs.

Now look at the performance of the patients (Figure 6.2). In the prehunch phase they kept choosing the bad packs. As already noted, there was no hunch phase. And perhaps most bizarrely of all, even when they had articulated that packs A and B were bad choices, they still picked more cards from those decks than from C and D! So despite "knowing" the correct conceptual answer, the lack of ability to feel emotion severely hampered their performance.

Similar games can be used to show that emotions can also handicap people without any emotional disconnect. Bechara et al.[7] play an investment game. Each player was given $20. They had to make a decision each round of the game: invest $1 or not invest. If the decision was not to invest, the task advanced to the next round. If the decision was to invest, players would hand over one dollar to the experimenter. The experimenter would then toss a coin in view of the player. If the outcome was heads, the player lost the dollar, if the coin landed tails up, then $2.50 was added to the player's account. The task would then move to the next round. Overall, twenty rounds were played.

Bechara et al. played this game with three different groups: (1) *normals*, (2) a group of players with damage to the neural circuitry associated with fear[8] (*target patients* who can no longer feel fear), and (3) a group of players with other lesions to the brain unassociated with the fear neural circuitry (*patient controls*).

The experimenters uncovered that the players with damage to the fear circuitry invested in 83.7 percent of rounds, the normals invested in 62.7 percent of rounds, and the patient controls 60.7 percent of rounds. Was this result attributable to the brain's handling of loss and fear? Figure 6.3 shows the results broken down based on the result in the previous round. It shows the proportions of groups that invested. It clearly demonstrates that normals and patient controls (those who showed more fear) were more likely to shrink away from risk-taking, both when they had lost in the previous round and when they won!

Players with damaged fear circuitry invested in 85.2 percent of

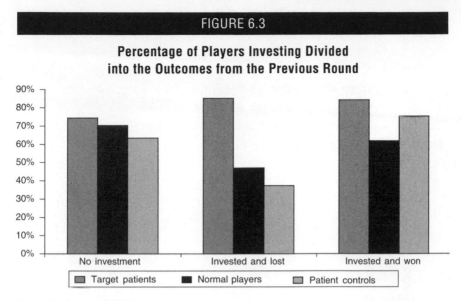

FIGURE 6.3

Percentage of Players Investing Divided into the Outcomes from the Previous Round

Source: Bechara et al. (2004)

rounds following losses on previous rounds, while normal players invested in only 46.9 percent of rounds following such losses.

Bechara et al. also found evidence of just how difficult learning actually is. Instead of becoming more optimal as time moves on, normal players actually become less optimal! (See Figure 6.4.) For the record, a rational player would, of course, play in all rounds.

So emotion can both help and hinder us. Without emotion we are unable to sense risk; with emotion, we can't control the fear that risk generates! Welcome to the human condition!

Camerer et al.[9] argue that the influence of emotions depends on the intensity of the experience:

> At low level of intensity, affect appears to play a largely "advisory" role. A number of theories posit that emotions carry information that people use as an input into the decisions they face . . .
>
> . . . At intermediate level of intensity, people begin to become conscious of conflicts between cognitive and affective

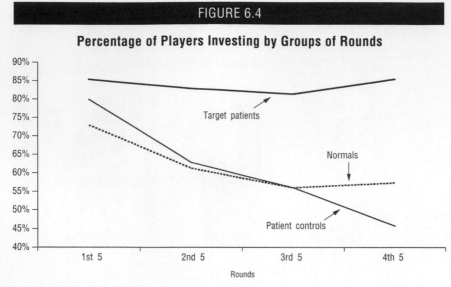

FIGURE 6.4

Percentage of Players Investing by Groups of Rounds

Source: Bechara et al. (2004)

inputs. It is at such intermediate levels of intensity that one observes . . . efforts at self-control . . .

. . . Finally, at even greater levels of intensity, affect can be so powerful as to virtually preclude decision-making. No one "decides" to fall asleep at the wheel, but many people do. Under the influence of intense affective motivation, people often report themselves as being "out of control" . . . As Rita Carter writes in Mapping the Mind, "where thought conflicts with emotion, the latter is designed by neural circuitry in our brains to win."

It is also worth noting that we are very bad at projecting how we will feel under the influence of emotion—a characteristic psychologists call hot–cold empathy gaps. That is to say, when we are relaxed and emotion free, we underestimate how we would act under the influence of emotion.

For instance, Loewenstein et al.[10] asked a group of male students to say how likely they were to act in a sexually aggressive manner in both a hot and cold environment, given a specific scenario. The scenario they were given concerned coming home with a girl they had picked up at a bar, having been told by friends that she had a reputation for being "easy." The story went on that the participants and the girl were beginning to get into physical genital contact on the sofa. The participants were then told they had started to try and remove the girl's clothes, and she said she wasn't interested in having sex.

Participants were then asked to assign probabilities as to whether they would (1) coax the girl to remove her clothes, or (2) have sex with her even after her protests. Figure 6.5 shows the self-reported probability of sexual aggressiveness (defined as the sum of the probabilities of 1 + 2). Under the no-arousal condition, there was an average 56 percent probability of sexual aggression. After having been shown sexually arousing photos, the average probability of aggression rose to nearly 80 percent!

SELF-CONTROL IS LIKE A MUSCLE

Unfortunately, a vast array of psychological research[11] suggests that our ability to use self-control to force our cognitive process to override

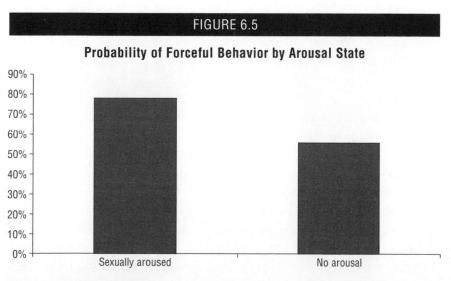

FIGURE 6.5

Probability of Forceful Behavior by Arousal State

Source: Loewenstein et al. (1997)

our emotional reaction is limited. Each effort at self-control reduces the amount available for subsequent self-control efforts.

A classic example of Baumeister's work concerns the following experiment. Participants were asked to avoid eating food for three hours before the experiment began (timed so they were forced to skip lunch). When they arrived, they were put into one of three groups.

The first group were taken into a room which cookies had recently been baked, so the aroma of freshly made chocolate chip delights wafted around. This room also contained a tray laid out with the freshly baked cookies and other chocolate delights, and a tray full of radishes. This group were told they should eat as many radishes as they could in the next five minutes, but they were also told they weren't allowed to touch the cookies. A second group was taken to a similar room with the same two trays, but told they could eat the cookies. The third group was taken to an empty room.

All the food was then removed and the individuals were given problems to solve. These problems took the form of tracing geometric shapes without retracing lines or lifting the pen from the paper. The problems were, sadly, unsolvable. However, the amount of time before participants gave up and the number of attempts made before they gave up were both recorded.

The results were dramatic. Those who had eaten the radishes (and had therefore expended large amounts of self-control in resisting the cookies) gave up in less than half the time that those who had eaten chocolate or eaten nothing had done. They also had far less attempts at solving the problems before giving up (see Figure 6.6).

Baumeister (2003)[12] concludes his survey by highlighting the key findings of his research:

1. Under emotional distress, people shift toward favoring high-risk, high payoff options, even if these are objectively poor choices. This appears based on a failure to think things through, caused by emotional distress.
2. When self-esteem is threatened, people become upset and lose their capacity to regulate themselves. In particular, people who hold a high opinion of themselves often get quite upset in re-

sponse to a blow to pride, and the rush to prove something great about themselves overrides their normal rational way of dealing with life.

3. Self-regulation is required for many forms of self-interest behavior. When self-regulation fails, people may become self-defeating in various ways, such as taking immediate pleasures instead of delayed rewards. Self-regulation appears to depend on limited resources that operate like strength or energy, and so people can only regulate themselves to a limited extent.

4. Making choices and decisions depletes this same resource. Once the resource is depleted, such as after making a series of important decisions, the self becomes tired and depleted, and its subsequent decisions may well be costly or foolish.

5. The need to belong is a central feature of human motivation, and when this need is thwarted such as by interpersonal rejection, the human being somehow ceases to function properly. Irrational and self-defeating acts become more common in the wake of rejection.

When I read this list it struck me just how many of these factors could influence investors. Imagine a fund manager who has just

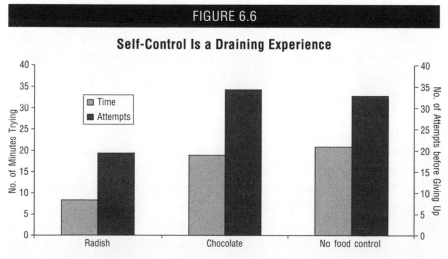

FIGURE 6.6

Self-Control Is a Draining Experience

Source: Baumeister et al. (1998)[13]

had a noticeable period of underperformance. This manager is likely to feel under pressure to start to focus on high-risk, high-payoff options to make up the performance deficit. He is also likely to feel his self-esteem is under threat, as outlined in point 2. The fund manager is also likely to begin to become increasingly myopic, focusing more and more on the short term. All of this is likely to be particularly pronounced if the position run resulting in the underperformance is a contrarian one. Effectively, pretty much all the elements that lead to the psychology of irrationality are likely to be present in large quantities.

PLASTICITY AS SALVATION

All of this may make for fairly depressing reading. With emotions we can't control ourselves, and without them we can't make decisions. We appear to be doomed to chase short-term rewards and run with the herd. When we try to resist these temptations, we suffer subsequent declines in our ability to exercise self-control. Not a pretty picture.

However, all is not lost. For many years it was thought that the number of brain cells was fixed and that they decayed over time. The good news is that this isn't the case. We are capable of generating new brain cells pretty much over our lifetime.

In addition, the brain isn't fixed into a certain format. The easiest way of thinking about this is to imagine the brain as a cobweb. Some strands of that cobweb are thicker than others. The more the brain uses a certain pathway, the thicker the strand becomes. The thicker the strand, the more the brain will tend to use that path. So if we get into bad mental habits, they can become persistent.

However, we are also capable of rearranging those pathways (neurons). This is how the brain learns. It is properly called *plasticity*. We aren't doomed; we can learn, but it isn't easy!

Perhaps the first step down this path is becoming aware of the fact that we are all likely to suffer from what psychologists call *heuristics and biases*. Heuristics are just rules of thumb that allow us to deal with informational deluge. In many cases they work well, but sometimes they lead us far astray from rational decision making.

Of course, we all like to think that we are immune to the influences of biases. But the reality is, of course, we are all likely to suffer some of these mental errors on some occasions. For instance, Pronin et al.[14] asked people to rate on a nine-point scale (with 5 being "somewhat") how likely the average American was to suffer a particular bias, and how likely they were to suffer the same biases. A booklet describing the biases was provided. Figure 6.7 shows the results. In all cases, people rated themselves less likely to suffer a given bias than average. Across the biases, the average score for the average American was 6.75. For those taking part, the average score was 5.31. All the differences were statistically significant. Pronin et al. refer to this as *bias blind spot.*

THE BIASES WE FACE

Psychologists have spent years documenting and cataloging the types of errors to which we are prone. The main results are surprisingly universal across cultures and countries.

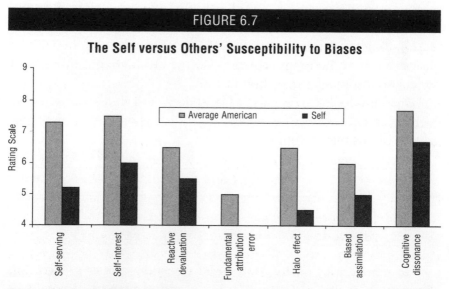

FIGURE 6.7

The Self versus Others' Susceptibility to Biases

Source: Adapted from Pronin et al. (2002)

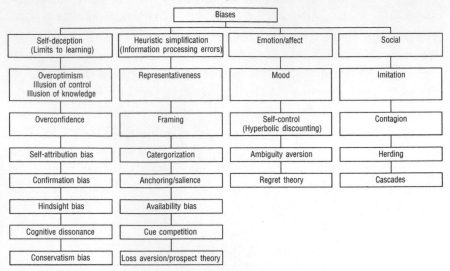

FIGURE 6.8

A Taxonomy of Biases

Source: DrKW Macro Research

Hirschleifer[15] suggests that most of these mistakes can be traced to four common causes: self-deception, heuristic simplification, emotion, and social interaction. Figure 6.8 tries to classify the major biases along these lines. It outlines the most common of the various biases that have been found, and also tries to highlight those with direct implications for investment.

This may look like a mass of mistakes, and indeed it is. However, for the purposes of exposition, let's focus on the ten most important biases that we come across.

BIAS #1
I know better, because I know more.

Let me start by asking you three questions. First, are you an above-average driver? Second, are you above average at your job? Third, are you above average as a lover?

So far in the countless times that I have conducted those questions I have only had one person answer that he is a below-average lover. For the record, he is one of my colleagues, and obviously desperately needs help! Now, why am I asking you these very strange questions? Well, they go to the heart of the two most common biases that we come across—*overoptimism* and *overconfidence*. Overoptimism and overconfidence tend to stem from the illusion of control and the illusion of knowledge.

The Illusion of Knowledge—More Information Isn't Better Information

The illusion of knowledge is the tendency for people to believe that the accuracy of their forecasts increases with more information. So dangerous is this misconception that Daniel Boorstin opined, "The greatest obstacle to discovery is not ignorance—it is the illusion of knowledge." The simple truth is that more information is not necessarily better information. It is what you do with it, rather than how much you have, that matters.

Nowhere is this better shown than in a classic study by Paul Slovic. Eight experienced bookmakers were shown a list of eighty-eight variables found on a typical past performance chart on a horse (e.g., the weight to be carried, the number of races won, the performance in different conditions etc.). Each bookmaker was then asked to rank the pieces of information by importance.

Having done this, the bookmakers were then given data for forty past races and asked to rank the top five horses in each race. Each bookmaker was given the past data in increments of the five, ten, twenty, and forty variables the bookmaker had selected as most important. Hence, each bookmaker predicted the outcome of each race four times—once for each of the information sets. For each prediction, the bookmakers were asked to give a degree of confidence ranking in their forecast.

Figure 6.9 shows how both accuracy and confidence change as the information set grows over time. Accuracy is pretty much a flat line regardless of the amount of information the bookmakers had at their disposal!

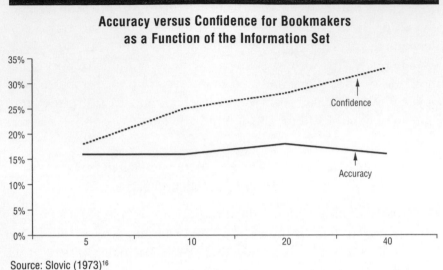

FIGURE 6.9

**Accuracy versus Confidence for Bookmakers
as a Function of the Information Set**

Source: Slovic (1973)[16]

However, look what happened to the bookmakers' confidence. It soared as the information set increased. With five pieces of information, accuracy and confidence were quite closely related. However, by the time forty pieces of information were being used, accuracy was still around 15 percent, but confidence has soared to more than 30 percent! So more information isn't better information; it is what you do with it that truly matters.

That fact doesn't stop the vast majority of investors desperately trying to accumulate more information than their rivals. The evidence suggests that, just like bookmakers, professional investors are generally much too confident.

Professionals: Worse than chance! Figure 6.10 is based on a new study by Torngren and Montgomery.[17] Participants were asked to select the stock they thought would do best each month from a pair of stocks. All the stocks were well-known blue-chip names, and players were given the name, industry, and prior twelve months' performance for each stock. Both laypeople (undergrads in psychology) and professional investors (portfolio managers, an-

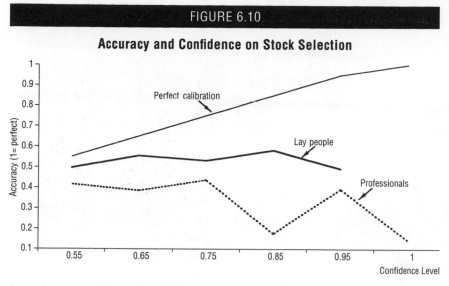

FIGURE 6.10

Accuracy and Confidence on Stock Selection

Source: Torngren and Montgomery (2004)

alysts, and brokers) took part in the study. At each selection, players were asked to state how confident they were in the outcome predicted.

The bad news is that both groups were worse than sheer luck. That is to say, you should have been able to beat both groups just by tossing a coin! The even worse news was that professionals were really dreadful, underperforming laypeople by a large margin. For instance, when the professionals were 100 percent sure they were correct, they were actually right less than 15 percent of the time! This fits with the mass of evidence that psychologists have uncovered that while experts may know more than non-experts, they are also likely to be even more overconfident than non-experts.

Players were also asked to rank the inputs they used in reaching their decisions. Figure 6.11 shows the average scores for the inputs. Laypeople were essentially just guessing, but were also influenced by prior price performance. In contrast, the professionals thought they were using their knowledge to pick the winners.

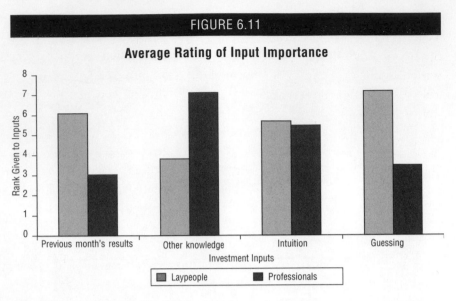

FIGURE 6.11

Average Rating of Input Importance

Source: Torngren and Montgomery (2004)

The Illusion of Control

The *illusion of control* refers to people's belief that they have influence over the outcome of uncontrollable events. For instance, people will pay four and a half times more for a lottery ticket that contains numbers they choose rather than a random draw of numbers. People are more likely to accept a bet on the toss of a coin before it has been tossed, rather than after it has been tossed and the outcome hidden, as if they could influence the spin of the coin in the air! Information once again plays a role. The more information you have, the more in control you will tend to feel.

BIAS #2

Big is the same as important.

Every piece of information can be judged along two dimensions—strength and weight. Confusing these two dimensions can easily generate overreaction and underreaction. For instance, let's assume you have interviewed a potential employee and have taken up his or her references. You receive a letter of recommendation, which is full of glowing testimonials to your potential employee's abilities in almost every walk of life. Sadly, the letter was written by the candidate's mom.

The strength of the information is represented by the high level of the glowing traits talked about; the weight of the information is very low because the author of the letter is a highly biased source.

Tversky and Griffin (1992)[18] have shown that, in general, a combination of high strength and low weight will generate overreaction, whereas low strength and high weight tends to create underreaction (see Table 6.4).

Investors often seem to confuse these two elements of information. For instance, when a firm announces either the introduction or suspension of a dividend payment, investors tend to underreact. They treat the information incorrectly. In fact, changes in dividend policy are very high weight (management doesn't alter dividend policy lightly). However, they also tend to be low strength because investors (incorrectly) don't place much emphasis on dividends.

In contrast, investors seem to almost continually overreact to firms with historically high earnings growth. Investors seem to take tremendous faith from a firm's past history, rather than focusing on the likely prospects in the future (more on this later).

TABLE 6.4

The Dimensions of Information

		Weight	
		High	Low
Strength	High	—	Overreaction
	Low	Underreaction	—

Source: DrKW Macro Research

BIAS #3

Show me what I want to see.

Consider the following situation: Four cards are laid out in front of you, and each card carries one alphanumeric symbol. The set comprises E, 4, K, 7. If I tell you that if a card has a vowel on one side, then it should have an even number on the other, which card(s) do you need to turn over to see if I am telling the truth?

Give it some thought. Most people go for E and 4. The correct answer is E and 7; only these two cards are capable of proving I am lying. If you turn the E over and find an odd number, then I was lying, and if you turn the 7 over and find a vowel then you know I was lying. By turning the 4 over you can prove nothing. If it has a vowel then you have found information that agrees with my statement but doesn't prove it. If you turn the 4 over and find a consonant, you have proved nothing. At the outset I stated a vowel must have an even number. I didn't say an even number must have a vowel!

So why are we drawn to the E and the 4? We have a very bad habit of looking for information that agrees with us. This thirst for agreement rather than refutation is known as *confirmatory bias*. When Karl Popper wrote about his philosophy of science, he stated that the only way of testing a view is to form the hypothesis and then spend the rest of the day looking for all the information that disagrees with us. But that isn't the way most of us work. We tend to form our views and then spend the rest of the day looking for all the data that make us look right.

Our natural tendency is to listen to people who agree with us. It feels good to hear our own opinions reflected back to us. We get those warm, fuzzy feelings of content. Sadly, this isn't the best way of making optimal decisions. What we should do is sit down with the people who disagree with us most. Not so we change our minds (because the odds are staked massively against such an outcome), but rather, so we become aware of the opposite point of view. We should look for the logical error in the opposite point of view. If we can't find such an error, then we shouldn't be so sure about holding our own view as strongly as we probably do.

A supplementary problem for trying to follow this path is that we often find ourselves suffering the *hostile media bias*. That is, not only do we look for information that agrees with us, but when we are presented with information that disagrees with us we tend to view the source as having a biased view!

BIAS #4

Heads was skill, tails was bad luck.

We have a relatively fragile sense of self-esteem; one of the key mechanisms for protecting this self-image is *self-attribution bias*. This is the tendency for good outcomes to be attributed to skill and bad outcomes to be attributed to sheer bad luck. This is one of the key limits to learning that investors are likely to encounter. This mechanism prevents us from recognizing mistakes as mistakes, and hence often prevents us from learning from those past errors.

To combat this problem we really need to use a matrix diagram similar to Table 6.5. Only by cross-referencing our decisions and the reasons for those decisions with the outcomes can we hope to understand where we are lucky and where we are skillful. That is, was I right for the right reason, or was I right for some spurious reason? In order to use this framework, we need a written record of the decisions we took and the reasoning behind those decisions, so remember to write things down.

TABLE 6.5

Decision Matrix

	Good Outcome	Bad Outcome
Right reason	Skill (could be luck, but let's be generous)	Bad luck
Wrong reason	Good luck	Mistake

BIAS #5

I knew it all along.

One of the most dangerous biases we encounter when teaching behavioral psychology is *hindsight bias.* This refers to the fact that after something has happened we are all really sure we knew about it beforehand! The best example of hindsight bias among investors is the dot-com bubble of the late 1990s. Going around talking with investors and telling them it was a bubble used to result in physical threats of violence against us. Yet now, going around seeing exactly the same set of investors, there has been an Orwellian rewriting of history. Now everyone sits there saying they knew it was a bubble—they were investing in it, but they knew it as a bubble!

Of course, if everyone thinks they can predict the past, they are likely to be far too sure about their ability to predict the future. Hence, hindsight is one of the dynamic generators of overconfidence. I mentioned that hindsight was one of the most dangerous biases when teaching behavioral psychology, because there is a risk that after reading this you will get up and walk away, saying, "Well, that was kind of interesting . . . but I knew it all along!"

BIAS #6

The irrelevant has value as input.

When faced with uncertainty we have a tendency to grab on to the irrelevant as a crutch. The incorporation of the irrelevant often happens without any conscious acknowledgment at all (a classic X-system trait).

The classic example of *anchoring* comes from Tversky and Kahneman's landmark paper.[19] They asked people to answer general knowledge questions, such as what percentage of the United Nations is made up of African nations? A wheel of fortune with the numbers 1 to 100 was spun in front of the participants before they answered. Being psychologists, Tversky and Kahneman had rigged the wheel so it gave either 10 or 65 as the result of a spin. The subjects were then asked if the answer was higher or lower than the number on the wheel, and also asked their actual answer. The median response from the group that saw the wheel spot at 10 was 25, and the median response from the group that saw 65 was 45! Effectively, people were grabbing at irrelevant anchors when forming their opinions. For what it is worth the percentage today is just under 20%.

Another well-known example concerns solving eight factorial (8!). It is presented in two different ways to the survey participants: as $1 \times 2 \times 3 \times 4 \times 5 \times 6 \times 7 \times 8$ or as $8 \times 7 \times 6 \times 5 \times 4 \times 3 \times 2 \times 1$. The median answer under the first scenario was 512; the median answer under the second scenario was 2,250. So people appear to anchor on the early numbers in forming their expectations. By the way, the actual answer is 40,320.

Anchoring has obvious implications for valuations, especially in a world in which we all sit in front of screens flashing prices at us all day long. It is far too easy to latch onto the current market price as an anchor. Analysts arc often fearful of announcing target prices that are a long way from current market prices. I know that, whenever I tell investors that the S&P 500 would need to fall to around 500 before I would be prepared to buy it, the reaction is usually a grin, like I have taken leave of my senses (which, in fairness, many have argued I did a long time ago). However, simply dismissing 500 because it is a long way from the current 1181 is a version of anchoring.

Northcraft and Neale[20] show that real estate agents suffer anchoring when pricing houses. They took two groups of real estate agents to the same house, and they gave them exactly the same information except that the original listing price of property was different for each group. They were asked to provide a variety of prices. The results are shown in Figure 6.12. On average, the difference between the two groups was more than 12 percent, despite the fact they looked at the same house!

A further example of anchoring affecting valuation can be found in a recent paper by Ariely, Loewenstein and Prelec.[21] In this study,

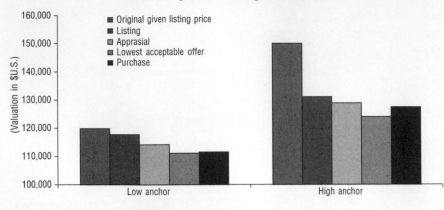

FIGURE 6.12

Anchoring and Housing Valuations

Source: Northcraft and Neale (1997)

participants were shown a variety of common(ish) objects. They were then asked whether they would buy the object for a dollar amount equal to the last two digits of their Social Security number. The participants were then asked the maximum price they would pay for each item. The idea of asking the first question was to set up the anchor (i.e., the last two digits of their Social Security number). If people anchor, then there should be some differences between those with a high/low Social Security number.

Figure 6.13 shows the results of Ariely et al.'s experiment. The average ratio of high Social Security number participants' maximum purchases prices to low Social Security number participants' maximum purchase prices was an incredible 2.7 times! The highest differential was just under 3.5 times. So, despite the fact that the Social Security numbers had nothing to do with the objects, they created vast valuation gaps.

The degree of anchoring is heavily influenced by the salience of the anchor. That is to say, the more seemingly relevant the anchor, the more people will tend to cling to it, which helps explain why analysts are so frequently afraid to have target prices that differ vastly from market prices. However, as already shown, even totally irrelevant anchors can have a massive effect on valuation.

FIGURE 6.13

Anchoring and Valuation (LHS is in $)

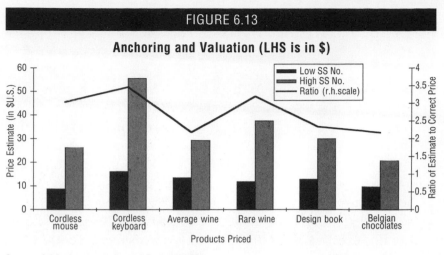

Source: Ariely, Loewenstein, and Prelec (2003)

From an aggregate market perspective, what are the likely anchors? Prices are flashed at us all day long—TV ads, newspaper inserts, ticker tape numbers scrolling across the bottom of the TV news channel, stock analysts' e-newsletters, real estate listings, and more. Investors seem to latch onto these price mirages and mistakenly equate them with values. Of course, we can guard against such mistakes by using reverse engineered models of valuation. Take market prices and back out what they imply for growth, and then assess whether there is any hope of that growth actually being delivered.

BIAS #7

I can make a judgment based on what it looks like.

Consider the following: Linda is 31, single, outspoken, and very bright. She majored in philosophy at her university, and as a student was deeply concerned with issues surrounding equality and discrimination. Is it more likely that Linda works in a bank, or is it more likely that Linda works in a bank and is active in the feminist movement?

Somewhat bizarrely, many people go for the latter option. But this can't possibly be true. The second option is a subset of the first option, and a subset can never be larger than one of the contributing sets!

So what is happening? Well, people judge events by how they appear, rather than by how likely they are. This is called *representativeness*. In the example of Linda, people picking the option that Linda works in a bank and is active in the feminist movement are underweighting the base rate that there are simply more people who work in banks than people who work in banks and are active in the feminist movement!

Representativeness has many applications in investment. For example, do investors think that good companies make good investments? If so, this is a potential case of representativeness. A further example of representativeness is outlined in Figure 6.14. It shows portfolios based around long-term earnings growth forecasts for consensus analysts.[22] The first bar shows the per-annum growth rate in the five years prior to expectation formation. It also traces out the earnings growth per annum in the one, three, and five years following the forecasts.

FIGURE 6.14

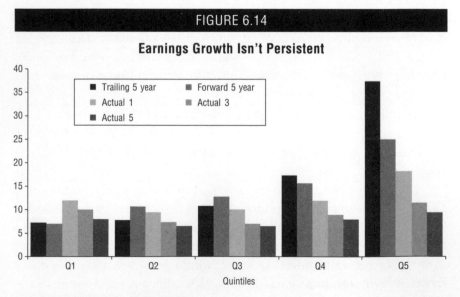

Earnings Growth Isn't Persistent

Source: DrKW, Montier, and Chan et al.[23]

The results show that analysts suffer representativeness twice over. First, companies that have seen high growth in the previous five years are forecast to continue to see very high earnings growth in the next five years. Analysts are effectively looking at the company's past performance and saying this company has been great, and hence it will continue to be great, or this company is a dog and it will always be a dog. This is exactly the same logic as the Linda problem!

Second, analysts fail to understand that earnings growth is a highly mean-reverting process over a five-year time period. The base rate for mean reversion is very high. The low-growth portfolio generates nearly as much long-term earnings growth as the high-growth portfolio. Effectively, analysts judge companies by how they appear, rather than how likely they are to sustain their competitive edge with a growing earnings base.

BIAS #8
That's not the way I remember it.

Our minds are not supercomputers, or even good filing cabinets. They bear more resemblance to post-it notes that have been thrown into the bin, and covered in coffee, which we then try to unfold and read! However, we all tend to think of our memories as perfect, like picture postcards or photos. The psychological truth is that memory is a mental process. One input into that process is the truth, but it is certainly not the only, let alone the major, input. In general, people are more likely to recall vivid, well-publicized, or recent information.

The *recency effect* is also reinforced by the fact that people tend to rely on their own experiences in preference to statistics or the experiences of others. In a wonderfully titled new paper—"The Tree of Experience in the Forest of Information"—Simonsohn et al.[24] show through a series of experiments that direct experience is frequently much more heavily weighted than general experience, even if the information is equally relevant and objective.

Simonsohn et al. hypothesize that one reason for the over-weighting of direct experience "is the impact of emotion. . . . [D]irectly experienced information triggers emotional reactions which vicarious information doesn't."

They continue, "If people use their direct experience to assess the likelihood of events, they are likely to overweight the importance of unlikely events that have occurred to them, and to underestimate the importance of those that have not." In fact, in one of their experiments, Simonsohn et al. find that personal experience is weighted twice as heavily as vicarious experience! All of this means that investors' experience will be a major determinant of their perception of reality.

The emotional impact of information also has its role to play. For instance, when asked which is a more likely cause of death in the United States, shark attacks or lightning strikes, a large number of people opt for shark attacks. Why? Because shark attacks are easy to recall, and they are easily available to the memory. When someone gets nibbled off the coast of Florida we all get to hear about it, and, to those of us of a certain age, *Jaws* was a truly terrifying film. In fact, the chances of being killed by a lightning strike are thirty times greater than the chance of getting killed by a shark. More people die each year from pig attacks or coconuts falling on their heads—or even getting their head stuck in an electric car door window—than die of shark attacks!

A less drastic example comes from Kahneman and Tversky (1973). They asked people the following: "In a typical sample of text in the English language, is it more likely that a word starts with the letter *k* or that *k* is its third letter?" Of the 152 people in the sample, 105 generally thought that words with the letter *k* in the first position were more probable. In reality, there are approximately twice as many words with *k* as the third letter as there are words that begin with *k*. Yet because we index on the first letter, we can recall them more easily.

The shark example has applications in finance. Investors are always looking for the big trigger event. However, in focusing on the big trigger, often investors miss the cumulative impact of small pieces of news. The press help perpetuate the myth that every infinitesimally small wiggle in the markets can be accounted for by some rational explanation. For instance, a recent paper contained the following explanation for a significant up day in the stock market: "U.S. stocks on Wednesday put up their best one-day showing in almost four months as falling crude prices and some positive corporate news bolstered the bulls in the lead up to the end of the first quarter."

> ## BIAS #9
>
> If you tell me it is so, it must be true.

WYSIWYG (pronounced *wizzy-wig*—what you see is what you get) was a computer term that described the on-screen appearance being identical to the printed version. All too often, financial data isn't WYSIWYG. *Obstrufication* (or obfuscation: confusion resulting from failure to understand) is frequently the name of the game when it comes to financial information. Of course, the financial markets employ a veritable army of analysts to check through the numbers and expose what is really going on. Well, that is the theory, at least!

However, the reality of analysis may be very different. I suspect that investors and analysts frequently suffer from narrow framing or frame dependence. That is to say, we simply don't see through the way in which information is presented to us. Any decent pollster can extract exactly the desired answer simply by framing the question in differing ways.

The following question represents a classic example of narrow framing:

Imagine that you are preparing for an outbreak of an unusual Asian disease that is expected to kill around 600 people. Two alternative programs to combat the disease have been proposed. Scientific estimates of the outcomes from the two programs are as follows:

If program A is adopted, 200 people will be saved.

If program B is adopted, there is a 1/3 probability that 600 people will be saved and a 2/3 probability that none of the 600 people will be saved.

Which program would you favor?

When Kahneman and Tversky asked this question they found that 72 percent of subjects favored Program A.

But now consider the same problem but with the following estimated outcomes:

If program C is adopted, 400 will die.

If program D is adopted, there is 1/3 probability that nobody will die, and 2/3 probability that 600 will die.

Kahneman and Tversky found that only 22 percent of subjects favored C.

Of course, the astute among you will have quickly spotted that program A is identical to program C, and program B is identical to program D. However, the way in which the question was presented created this oddity of preference reversal.

The importance of framing is probably due to cognitive limits. Our brains are not supercomputers; they have only limited ability to deal with information. In particular, we tend to suffer from something known as *inattentional blindness*.[25] Inattentional blindness is a phenomenon in which people fail to notice stimuli appearing in front of their eyes when they are preoccupied with an attentionally demanding task.

My favorite example involves people being asked to watch two groups of players (one dressed in white, the other dressed in black) pass a basketball between members of their own team. Watchers are asked to count the number of passes between players wearing white tops. They were also asked to note if anything unusual occurs during the watching of the video. As the film is played, a gorilla walks into view, faces the camera and beats his chest. Despite the obvious incongruity of this occurring, 46 percent of watchers failed to notice anything out of the ordinary![26]

Let me give you an example from the field of finance. We are frequently told that repurchases have surpassed dividends as a method of distributing cash to shareholders. Indeed, a quick glance at Figure 6.15 would seem to decisively answer in the affirmative.

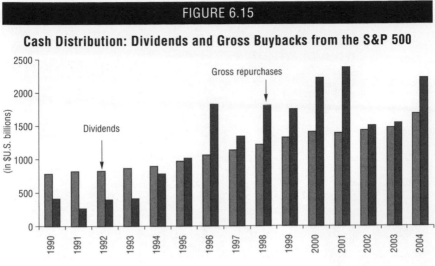

FIGURE 6.15

Cash Distribution: Dividends and Gross Buybacks from the S&P 500

Source: DrKW Macro Research

However, the clue as to why this may be a highly misleading statement is in the title to the chart. It shows gross buybacks, or announced buybacks. However, simply because a firm announces a buyback doesn't mean that it is going to carry out a repurchase.

In fact, since 1987 completed buybacks have been running at just 57 percent of the announced level. Those determined to look for good news can (perhaps) take some comfort in the fact that thus far in 2005, completed buybacks are running at the rate of 80 percent of announced buybacks.

However, even completed buybacks aren't really of interest to us as continuing shareholders. The only thing that matters to me as a continuing shareholder is the net level of buybacks—that is, buybacks after accounting for the equity issuance that goes on (largely related to stock options). Sadly, on average net buybacks represent only 19 percent of announced buybacks. Once again, this figure has been higher of late, running at the rate of 35 percent in 2005 (see Figure 6.16).

We are now in a position to assess the impact of repurchases on the distributions to shareholders. In Figure 6.17 I've converted all the figures into yield equivalents. Even a cursory glance reveals that

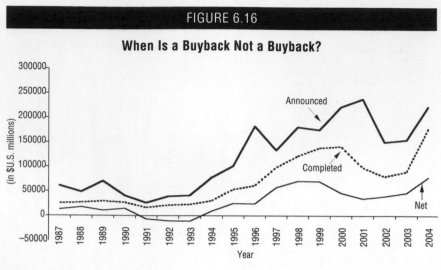

FIGURE 6.16

When Is a Buyback Not a Buyback?

Source: DrKW Macro Research

repurchases have not even come close to compensating investors for the declines in dividend yields witnessed during the long bull market. If net repurchases continue to run at current rates, then buybacks will add 76 basis points (bps) to the dividend yield this year, taking the overall yield to 2.4 percent—hardly the sort of levels to fire the imagination.

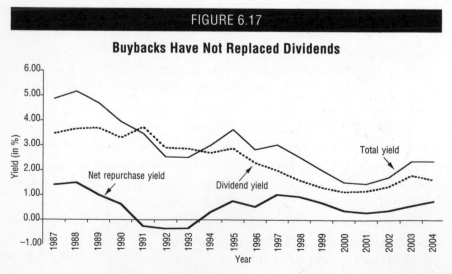

FIGURE 6.17

Buybacks Have Not Replaced Dividends

Source: DrKW Macro Research

BIAS #10
A loss isn't a loss until I take it.

Imagine you had bought a bottle of wine for $15 a few years ago. The wine has now appreciated vastly in price so that at auction a bottle would now fetch something north of $150. Would you be prepared to buy a bottle or sell your existing stock? The most frequently encountered answer is a resounding no to both questions. When faced with this situation, people are generally unwilling to either buy or sell the wine.

This inaction inertia is known as *the status quo bias* (which is not a bizarre attachment to an aging rock group as some may think). It is also an example of the *endowment effect*. Simply put, the endowment effect says that once you own something you start to place a higher value on it than others would.

The endowment effect is relatively easy to demonstrate empirically. The classic format is to randomly give half a class of students a mug (say). Then tell the class that a market will be formed in which students with mugs can sell them to students without mugs who might want them. Presumably, since the mugs were randomly distributed, roughly half the people should wish to trade. So the predicted volume level is 50 percent.

However, volumes in such markets are usually a fraction of that which might be expected. Indeed, in many experiments the actual volume level is closer to 10 percent! The key reason for the lack of transactions is a massive gap between the would-be buyers and sellers.

Figure 6.18 shows the results from a typical experiment.[27] The object issued was indeed university mugs (a staple in such experiments). These mugs retailed for $6 at the university store. Those who had mugs were willing to sell them from $5.25 on average (known as the willingness to accept, or WTA). Those who didn't have mugs weren't willing to spend more than $2.50 to acquire one (known as the willingness to pay, or WTP).

So, despite being given the mugs only minutes before, the act of ownership led sellers to ask for double the amount that buyers

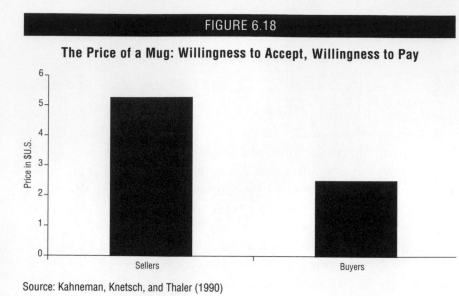

FIGURE 6.18

The Price of a Mug: Willingness to Accept, Willingness to Pay

Source: Kahneman, Knetsch, and Thaler (1990)

were willing to actually pay for the mug. Ownership seems to massively distort people's perceptions of value.

Does this endowment effect stem from a reluctance to buy or a reluctance to sell? The relative importance of these two factors can be assessed by introducing a third category of player into the market. Rather than having just buyers and sellers, experimenters have introduced *choosers*. As before, mugs are distributed across the class randomly. The sellers were asked if they would be willing to sell their mugs at prices ranging from $0.25 to $9.25. A second group, the buyers, were asked if they would be willing to buy a mug over the same range of prices. A third group, the choosers, were not given a mug but were asked to choose, for each of the prices, whether they would rather receive a mug or the amount of money.

In theory, the choosers and the sellers are in exactly the same situation—both groups are deciding at each price between the mug and the amount of money. The only difference between the two groups is that the choosers don't have physical possession of a mug. However, Figure 6.19 shows the theory doesn't really count for very much!

FIGURE 6.19

The Price of a Mug: Sellers, Choosers, and Buyers

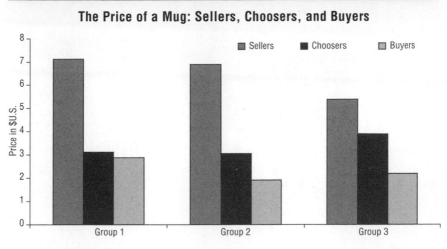

Source: KKT (1990) and Franciosi et al. (1996)

Across three different experiments at three different universities the choosers seem to act much more like buyers than sellers. Across the experiments reported here,[28] choosers' prices were generally higher (on average around 50 percent higher) than the buyers' prices, but still well below the prices set by the sellers. Sellers had prices that were on average nearly three times greater than the buyers were willing to pay, and nearly double the amount the choosers would have been willing to trade at.

This represents clear evidence of the endowment effect being driven by a reluctance of the owner to part with their endowment, even though they may have only actually owned the item in question for a matter of minutes.

Think about these effects the next time you're considering a particular company. If you already hold stock in that company, you may actually impute a higher value than is warranted, simply because you already own the shares. You are likely to enter a meeting with company management looking to be convinced that any concerns you had are misplaced. Of course, management will never tell you anything other than it is a great business and a great investment.

Some very successful fund managers never ever see companies for this very reason.

Rather than walking into the meeting in a skeptical frame of mind thinking "unless I hear something that really alters my view then I will sell this stock," we tend to look for all the information that agrees with our stance, which, when we already own a stock, is likely to be "I'll keep holding this stock."

Both the status quo bias and the endowment effect are part of a more general issue known as *loss aversion*. Psychologists long ago noted that people tend to worry about gains and losses rather than about levels (in direct violation of normal economic theory).[29] In particular, people have been found to dislike losses far more than they like gains.

For example, consider the following: You are offered a bet on the toss of a fair coin. If you lose, you must pay me £100. What is the minimum amount that you need to win in order to make this bet attractive?

Unlike many of the questions from psychology that have graced these pages, this one has no right or wrong answer. It is purely a matter of personal choice. Figure 6.20 shows the answers I received when I played this game with some former colleagues from another investment bank.

The average response was well over £200. That fits with all the studies that have been done on loss aversion. In general, people seem to dislike loss 2 to 2.5 times as much as they enjoy gains.

Shefrin and Statman[30] predicted that because people dislike incurring losses much more than they enjoy making gains, and people are willing to gamble in the domain of losses, investors will hold onto stocks that have lost value (relative to the reference point of their purchase) and will be eager to sell stocks that have risen in value. Effectively, they argued people tended to ride losers and cut winners. This has become known as the *disposition effect*.

Odean[31] obtained data from a discount brokerage for around 10,000 accounts from 1987 to 1993. Each purchase and sale for each account had been recorded. Odean found that investors held losing stocks for a median 124 days and held winning stocks for a median of 102 days. He also calculated the percentage of losing positions

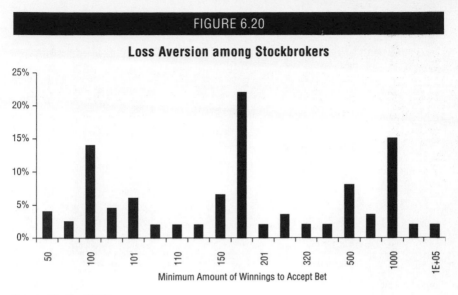

FIGURE 6.20

Loss Aversion among Stockbrokers

Minimum Amount of Winnings to Accept Bet

Source: Montier (2002)

that were realized (as a percentage of all losing stocks held) and the percentage of winning positions that were realized (as a percentage of all winning stocks held).

Lo and behold, Odean uncovered that these individual investors sold an average of 15 percent of all winning positions and only 9 percent of all losing positions. That is to say, individual investors are 1.7 times as likely to sell a winning stock than a losing stock (see Figure 6.21).

One of the most common reasons for holding onto a stock is the belief that it will bounce back subsequently. This could be motivated by any number of potential psychological flaws ranging from overoptimism and overconfidence to self-attribution bias (a belief that good outcomes are the result of skill, and bad outcomes are the result of sheer bad luck). Odean decided to investigate whether investors were correctly betting on recovery in the losers that they continued to hold. Sadly, he found the winners that were sold outperformed the losers that continued to be held by an average excess return of 3.4 percent a year.

Odean[32] has also studied the behavior of investors in mutual

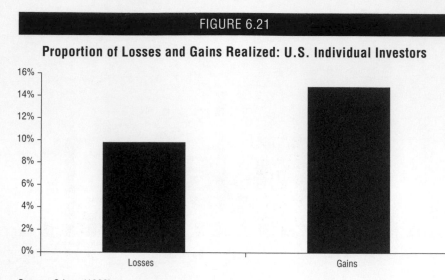

FIGURE 6.21

Proportion of Losses and Gains Realized: U.S. Individual Investors

Source: Odean (1998)

funds (rather than direct shares). This time the period covered 1990 to 1996 and encompassed some 32,000 households with holdings of mutual funds. Odean uncovered a very similar pattern to the evidence already presented. When it comes to buys, some 54 percent of investors' purchases are in the top 20 percent of mutual funds ranked by past performance (that is to say, investors chase past winners). However, when it comes to selling mutual funds, only 14 percent of all investors' sales are in the bottom 20 percent of mutual funds ranked by past performance. In fact, it transpires that mutual fund investors were more than 2.5 times as likely to sell a winning fund rather than a losing fund (see Figure 6.22).

Professional investors are often very dismissive of such findings. In general, they assume that all of this behavioral finance malarkey applies to individual investors but not to them. This seems to be a classic example of that key behavioral characteristic—overconfidence.

However, such overconfidence looks to be sadly misplaced. Andrea Frazzini[33] has recently investigated the behavior of mutual fund managers, and he has uncovered that even such seasoned professionals seem to suffer loss aversion.

Frazzini analyzed the holding and transactions of mutual funds

FIGURE 6.22

Proportion of Buys and Sells Across Best and Worst Funds

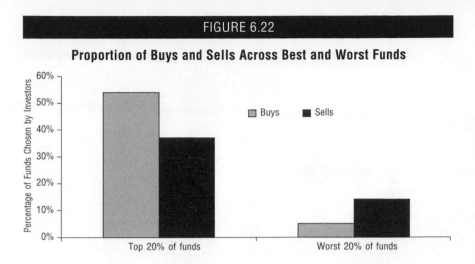

between 1980 and 2002. He ends up with a sample of nearly 30,000 U.S. domestic mutual funds. Just like Odean, he finds that professional money managers seem to suffer loss aversion. Across all funds, he found that 17.6 percent of all gains were realized, but only 14.5 percent of all losses were realized. So professional investors were 1.2 times as likely to sell a winning stock rather than a losing stock.

However, Frazzini takes his analysis one step further. He ranks the mutual funds by the performance achieved over the last twelve months. The results are shown in Figure 6.23. The best-performing funds are those with the highest percentage of losses realized (i.e., the least loss averse). The best-performing funds are less than 1.2 times more likely to sell a winning position than a losing position.

The worst-performing funds had the lowest percentage of realized losses. In fact, the worst-performing funds show about the same degree of loss aversion as the individual investors. They are 1.7 times more likely to sell a winning position than a losing position.

Investors would be well advised to be mindful of this strong evidence of loss aversion. As with all biases, everyone is likely to think that they are less likely than everyone else to suffer from loss

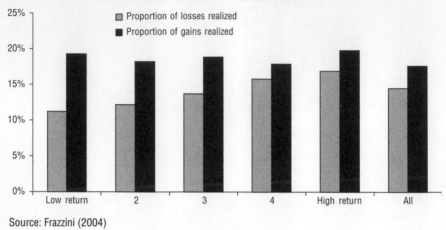

FIGURE 6.23

Proportion of Losses and Gains Realized:
U.S. Domestic Mutual Funds

Source: Frazzini (2004)

aversion. The reality of the situation is that we all seem to be liable to the fear of loss. As such a (formal) sell discipline is likely to be of prime importance within any successful investment process.

CONCLUSIONS

These ten biases seem to be the most common mental pitfalls that investors stumble into. The following fifteen rules are attempts to suggest ways in which we might try and avoid plunging headlong into them:

1. These biases apply to me, you, and everyone else as well.
2. You know less than you think you do.
3. Try to focus on the facts, not the stories.
4. More information doesn't equal better information.
5. Think whether a piece of information is high strength and low weight, or low strength and high weight.
6. Look for information that disagrees with you.

7. Your failures aren't just bad luck; examine mistakes to improve performance.
8. You didn't know it all along, you just think you did.
9. If you can't debias, then rebias—we know people will anchor on the irrelevant, so let's replace the unimportant with the relevant. Set up a sensible valuation framework.
10. Judge things by how statistically likely they are, not how they appear.
11. Don't overweight personal experience.
12. Big, vivid, easy to recall events are less likely than you think they are.
13. Don't take information at face value; think carefully about how it was presented to you.
14. Don't value something more, simply because you own it.
15. Sell your losers and ride your winners.

Of course, these may all seem very obvious. However, a little like New Year's resolutions, they are easy to say and hard to implement. Having an investment process that incorporates best mental practice requires you to step back from the hurly burly of day-to-day market turbulence and understand how to apply psychology's findings to your own behavior.

CHAPTER 7

The Means Are the Ends

Bill Bonner is the president and CEO of Agora publishing, one of the largest financial newsletter companies. It is headquartered in Baltimore with offices in London, Paris, Ireland, Bonn, and Johannesburg. Bill is also the creator and key contributor to The Daily Reckoning, *the contrary financial newsletter sent out via e-mail (www.dailyreckoning.com). The newsletter now has more than 500,000 readers and is translated from English into German and French. Bill is also the co-author of the best-selling* Financial Reckoning Day.

Bill is the father of six great kids. He (along with his wife, Elizabeth) moved the entire group to Paris to give them a view of life outside America and to learn new languages. Most of them now speak at least two or three fluently. He then bought a chateau (also known as a pile of old stones) in the south of France at Ouzilly. He then enlisted his kids on summers and weekends to help him restore it. I have had the pleasure of visiting him on several occasions and marveling at his ability to get his kids to work. If he can just put his secret into a research report, it would become extremely popular.

Bill is one of my favorite writers. I have often said I feel like a house painter in front of a Rembrandt while reading his prose. He is an iconoclastic reader and thinker with a strong libertarian bent, mixed in with Austrian economics. Bill was in one of his cynical moments, thinking about governments and economics, when he wrote a particularly humorous and thought-provoking essay. Here, in its edited version, is Bill's take on the folly of government meddling with the economy.   —John Mauldin

The Means Are the Ends

by Bill Bonner

∾

ECONOMICS HAS BEEN CALLED THE *DISMAL SCIENCE*. BUT EVEN THAT IS MERELY fraud and flattery. Economics *is* dismal, but it isn't science. At its best it is merely voyeurism—peeping into people's windows as they go about their business, trying to figure out what they are doing. At worst, it is pompous theorizing about how to get the schmucks to do better.

We doubt that you are especially interested in economics, dear reader. We know we are not. But we are giving advice; economists can help us find it. Besides, we can't resist a good comedy . . . or a good opportunity to point and giggle. We keep our eye on economists and politicians the way children watch clowns; we can't wait to see them get whacked in the head or trip over each other.

But what is amusing is also instructive. Are not clowns people, too? Are they not part of human life . . . human organization . . . and human economy? Economists, like politicians, are driven by the same motors that power everyone else. Some want power, others glory, others money—and some want all three. But how do they get it? Can we not watch politicians and economists and learn something about ourselves?

One of the many conceits of politicians and economists is that they are somehow out of the ordinary. They are godlike, or so they pretend, with the power to look into the future and improve it before it happens. No sparrow can fall in a deserted patch of earth without it registering, somehow, on their meters and troubling their sensitive souls. For they claim no other ambition but to make the world a better place. Neither drink, nor meat, nor false witness cross their lips. They sweat for no material gain and know no lust—save for the betterment of all mankind. They pass laws and enact codes and regulations as if they were the masters of the whole human race, tinkering with it from a distance until they get it right. Since they float above it all, they are not subject to the normal temptations, while the rest of us spend our whole lives like raccoons searching for a garbage pail without a lid. Unless we are kept in tight cages, who knows what we will do?

But thank God there are leaders! Thinkers! Theorists with their "isms," and their rat wire . . . ready not merely to keep us from hurting one another, but also to give us a sense of moral purpose. It is not enough that we should each seek happiness in our own private way, we must free the Sudetenland! Abolish poverty! Make the world safe for democracy! We must realize our manifest destiny . . . and provide *Lebensraum* (living space) for the German people! Full employment! A minimum wage! No humbug left behind!

We bring this up to laugh at it—and to reach for instruction. We are taught to admire leaders and opinion setters without being told that almost all they say is self-serving claptrap and most of what they do is counterproductive, fraudulent, and sometimes lethal. But we realize, intuitively, that they are mere mortals. That is why we get such perverse joy when the press reports that some government official has been caught having an affair with his secretary, or some public figure is convicted of embezzling.

KEYNESIAN MEDDLING IN THE TWENTIETH CENTURY

In the early twentieth century, John Maynard Keynes came up with a new idea about economics. Keynes argued that a government could take the edge off a business recession by making more credit available when money got tight—and by spending more money itself to make up for the lack of spending on the part of consumers and businessmen. He suggested, whimsically, hiding bottles of cash all around town, where boys might find them, spend the money, and revive the economy. The politicians loved it; Keynes had explained how they could meddle in private affairs on a grand scale.

The new idea caught on. Soon economists were advising all major governments about how to implement the new *ism*. It did not seem to bother anyone that the new system was a scam. Where would this new money come from? Whose money was it? And if the owner of the money thought it best to save it, rather than spend it, what made economists think they knew better? All the Keynesians had done was to substitute their own guesses for the private, personal, economic decisions of millions of ordinary citizens—and their own phony money and credit for the real thing. They had resorted to what Franz Oppenheimer called *political means*, instead of allowing normal *economic means* to take their own course.

There are only two ways to get what you want in life, dear reader. There are honest means, and dishonest ones. There are economic means, and there are political means. There is persuasion . . . and there is force. There are civilized ways . . . and barbaric ones. Economists are just harmless cranks as long as they are just peeping through the window. But when they undertake to get people to do what they want—either by offering them money that is not their own, by defrauding them with artificially low interest rates, or by printing up money that is not backed by something of real value (such as gold) they have moved to political means to accomplish their goals. They have crossed over to the dark side.

Keynesian "improvements" were first applied in the 1920s when Fed Governor Ben Strong decided to give the U.S. economy a little *coup de whiskey* by lowering interest rates, making money cheap, and pouring a little fuel onto the already hot stock market. They were tried again in the 1930s when the economy was recovering from the hangover. The results were predictably disastrous. And along came other economists with apologies, explanations, and bad ideas of their own. Rare was the man, such as Robert Lucas or Murray Rothbard, who pointed out that you could not really improve economic results with political means.

If a national assembly could make people rich simply by passing laws, we would all be billionaires already. Political assemblies have passed a multitude of laws and seem capable of enacting any piece of legislation brought before them. If laws could make people wealthy, some assembly somewhere would have found the magic edicts—simply by chance. But instead of making them richer, each law makes people a little poorer. Every time political means are used, they interfere with the private, civilized economic arrangements that actually get people what they want. One man makes shoes. Another grows potatoes. The potato grower goes to the cobbler to buy a pair of shoes. He must exchange two sacks of potatoes for one pair of penny loafers. But then the meddlers show up and tell the cobbler he must charge three sacks so that he can pay one in taxes to the meddlers themselves. And then he needs to put an alarm system in his shop, buy a hardhat, pay his helper minimum wage, and fill out forms for all manner of laudable purposes. When the potato farmer finally shows up at the cobbler's, he is informed that the shoes will cost seven sacks of potatoes! That is just what the cobbler has to charge in order to end up with the same two sacks he needed to charge in the beginning. "No thanks," says the potato man, "At that price, I can't afford a pair of shoes."

What the potato grower needs, say the economists, is more money! The money supply has failed to keep pace, they add. That was why they urged the government to set up the Federal Reserve in the first place; they wanted a stooge currency that would go along with their goofy plans. Gold is fine, they said, but it's antisocial. It resists progress and drags its feet on financing new social programs. Why, it is positively recalcitrant! Clearly, when we face a war or a Great National Purpose we need money that is more patriotic. Gold malingers. Gold hesitates. Gold is reticent. Gold keeps to itself, offering neither advice nor encouragement. What we need is a more public-spirited money—a source of public funding, a flexible, expandable national currency, a *political money* that we can work with. We need a dollar that is not linked to gold.

In the many years since the creation of the Federal Reserve System as America's central bank, gold has remained as steadfast and immobile as ever. An ounce of it today buys about the same amount of goods and services as an ounce in 1913. But the dollar has gone along with every bit of political gimcrackery that has come along—the war in Europe, the New Deal, WWII, the Cold War, the Vietnam War, the war on poverty, the war on illiteracy, the New Frontier, the Great Society, Social Security, Medicare, Medicaid, the war in Iraq, the war on terror . . . the list is long and sordid. As a result, guess how much a dollar is worth today in comparison to one in 1913? Five cents.

Keynesianism is a fraud. Supply-siderism is a con. The dollar it-self is a scam. All were developed by people with good intentions, but these good intentions not only paved the road to hell, they greased it. There was no point putting on the brakes. Once under-way, there was no stopping.

Right now, the United States might be sliding toward some sort of hell. A half-century of deceit has produced a population as cred-ulous as its money. Americans are ready to believe anything—and go along with anything. But they will be very disappointed when they discover that all the political means they counted on—the phony money, the laws, the regulations, the wars—have made them poorer. That is when we will really need cages.

MORALITY AS AN ECONOMIC TOOL

"Nothing in nature is evil," said Marcus Aurelius. Keynes was hu-man. Even Adolph Hitler was a man, a part of nature himself. And the Evil Empire—was it not created by men too, men who like economists and politicians followed their own natural impulses? Adolph may have erred and strayed. Hitler thought he was building a better world, and he could argue all day that his plan was the best way forward.

Not that there weren't arguments on the other side. German universities were among the finest in the world. Some argued that German scientists and philosophers were the best the world had to offer. What did all these smart people think? They thought all kinds of things—and argued the relative merits of one plan over another. Jews were a nuisance, said some. Jews were good merchants, said others. We must defeat Russia, many believed. Avoid a two-front war, thought others. There were so many thoughts available, peo-ple could think anything they wanted.

What would an observer think? No amount of logic could dis-suade Hitler from his chosen course. So what is an observer to do? The preacher would say, "Love the sinner but hate the sin." That is a useful point. There is no point hating Hitler—or Stalin, or Osama—they are God's creatures, too, just like the rest of us.

Of course, God's creatures have a certain consensus about what constitutes heinous sin. It is fairly cut and dried to say that genocide is a bad thing.

People argued about Keynesianism for many years, too. If we were to give one piece of advice to a young person—or even an old person—what better counsel could be offered than to avoid arrogance? It is such vanity that makes a politician strut and crow . . . and an economist paw the earth. It is vanity that makes him presume that his plans are so important, so beneficent, that they should override the plans of millions of others. It is vanity that makes him think that he knows better than other adults what they should do with their lives and their money.

And yet, we all like to look at our own faces in the mirror. That is human, too. And without that necessary arrogance, how will the politician ever get his name in the paper? Would he not live in the shadows of great men all his life? Would he be considered a nice guy, to be walked all over in business and ignored at cocktail parties? Would his rivals not get elected to high office, run major corporations, and marry trophy wives? Even if thoughtful people regard him as a pompous buffoon, isn't this "great man" the winner in the eyes of many?

If only the world were simpler. If only people whom we thought deserved to win always did win! If only the buffoons carried signs around their necks, rather than medals on their chests.

And yet, we cling to a stubborn faith and dumb observation that modesty is a virtue and virtue is rewarded and vice punished. We have seen how vice is punished in the public sphere. When an economist crosses over to the dark side and begins telling other people what to do, the result is always and everywhere complete disaster. Economic disaster is merely the most humane example. Economists cost people a lot of money, but what is money compared to the millions of people murdered, enslaved, starved to death, or imprisoned in the name of making the world a better place? People tend to underestimate, wrote French historian Raymond Aron, "the persistence of history's traditional side, the rise and fall of empires, the rivalry of regimes, the disastrous or beneficent exploits of great men."

The names of the "great men" are recorded in history books and chiseled in granite. We know of no examples of "beneficent exploits," so we presume Aron was being sarcastic. Of disastrous exploits, on the other hand, the history books are full: Genghis Khan, Tamerlane the Great, Caesar, Alexander . . . and more recently, Mussolini, Wilson, Hitler, Bush . . . few national leaders fail to make the list. For all have their desired "improvements," and nearly all are ready to resort to violence to see them realized.

Is the world a better place for all their bloody efforts? We don't know. Alas, you can never know where your actions will lead, or what will happen next in the world around you. So, what is a person to do? All you can do is to become engaged in the struggle for a better world, say the existentialists. But that is what all the world improvers and "Great Leaders" do. We have other advice: Mind your own business.

"I beseech you in the bowels of Christ to consider that you may be wrong," wrote Oliver Cromwell to the General Assembly of the Church of Scotland in 1650.

In public life, you may be wrong more often than not. If your advice involves forcing someone else to do something . . . or deceiving them into doing it . . . or any other political means of getting what you want, you are almost certainly wrong. For you are merely interrupting someone else's private ambitions—and his economic means of realizing them. Nothing much can be done to improve on the private arrangements of millions of free people. There are no better means for people to get what they want than the economic means—that is, the private, civilized, voluntary arrangements that they work out among themselves. Any attempt to interfere with these private deals, trades, and programs inevitably causes problems. People already know what they want. Their private arrangements are all designed to help them get it. All the leader can do is to divert them away from getting what they actually want toward some theoretical good that, in the end, always turns out to be bad for everyone.

A modest man would not presume to tell other adults what to do. He feels lucky to be able to direct his own activities, let alone give orders to millions of others. He is never completely sure he's doing the right thing. But in his own, private world he is the one who pays the price for his mistakes; as soon as he recognizes them, he usually corrects them quickly—or, if he is bent for self-destruction, gets what he is after. He may or may not realize his ambitions, but as long as he sticks to economic means, at least he won't go to Hell.

The Great Leader, by contrast, never doubts that he is making a better world. Even when the evidence piles up all around, as it did around Hitler in his 1945 bunker, he is still sure that he did the right thing. When things go wrong, he blames his subordinates as incompetent and ungrateful. Hitler was so disappointed by the ingratitude of the German people that he came to feel they were not worthy of his improvement efforts. The Third Reich failed, he said, because they were unwilling to give it the sacrifices it needed. Now that the Russian army was entering Berlin and the German population was starving, they deserved to suffer, said he.

The real problem of the Great Leader is the same problem as with the little follower—and the problem we all face. All humans want more or less the same things—power, money, prestige, status. Getting them by civilized means—that is, working for them, earning them, deserving them—is a long and difficult process. Nor is there ever any guarantee that lightning won't strike you dead just before you get where you are going. That is why the temptation to cheat—to take up dishonest, political shortcuts—is almost irresistible.

If you meet a pretty woman and you know you will never see her again, what do you have to lose? You may want to have your way with her—using seductive lies or maybe brute force—that is, if you are a cad. But if you think you will have to live with her for the rest of your life, you will be more careful. Force and fraud won't work for long. You will need something else. The qualities that are useful in politics, war, and adultery—being strong, smart, unpredictable, and able to lie with a straight face—are the very same qualities that often get you into trouble in the rest of life.

We're not smart enough to know whether one person's plan for world improvement will actually make the place better. All we know is whether the means the person uses are civilized. That is the problem with history's monsters—its great leaders, its world improvers, its gigolos, central bankers, and connivers. Not that they had outrageous ideas, but that they resorted to political means to get what they wanted. But we do not hate them; we just hope they get what they deserve.

"Bad boys" may get the girls, but they have trouble keeping them. Good husbands, on the other hand, may be boring, but a smart woman treasures one as she would a set of old china. Likewise, a businessman can cheat his customers and gain a temporary advantage. So can a Great Leader invade a neighbor and seem to be on top of the world—for a while. A grump, annoyed by his neighbor's trash, might decide to shoot the man. Or a woman, irritated by her husband, might decide to run the man down. These are all solutions to problems. But in every case, resorting to political means to achieve the ends they craved took them over to the dark side of life. They are no longer doing civilized things, but barbaric ones. They are doing the things the Baptist preachers tell you to hate. They are doing the things that bring bad karma . . . things the gods punish . . . and things that make other men seek revenge.

For all we know, of course, all these stories will have happy endings. The woman who ran over her husband might be delighted with the results. The businessman might take the profits he made from cheating his customers and use them to make a killing on Wall Street. It is not for us to know how things work out.

The ends are beyond us. We never know what will happen. Nor do we know what God's Own Plan may be—either for us, or for the world itself. All we have is the means. That is all we control. But if we use the means of civilized people—the economic means—to get what we want, we will not necessarily get what we want, but at least we will deserve it.

CHAPTER 8

The 2 Percent Solution

∽

Rob Arnott is one of those guys who—with few exceptions—becomes the smartest guy in the room just by walking into it. He is chairman of Research Affiliates, runs an $8 billion fund for Pimco (which will probably be $10 billion by the end of 2005), manages a few hedge funds, and is launching a new index fund or two. He is also the editor of the Financial Analysts Journal, *one of the most prestigious publications on investments and finance. Rob has authored more than sixty articles for journals such as the* Financial Analysts Journal, *the* Journal of Portfolio Management, *and the* Harvard Business Review. *He has been awarded not one but five Graham and Dodd Scrolls awards, awarded annually by the CFA Institute (formerly AIMR), and two Bernstein-Fabozzi/Jacobs-Levy awards, awarded by the* Journal of Portfolio Management *and* Institutional Investor, *for the best articles of the year. For financial analysts, this is the equivalent of being selected the MVP in the major leagues.*

Rob is a wine connoisseur (thus, it is always a good idea to go to his home to discuss ideas late in the evening). He collects vintage motorbikes and is a good friend. Here, he tells us how to get 2 percent more a year out of the stock market simply by restructuring our portfolios. —John Mauldin

∽

The 2 Percent Solution

by Rob Arnott

❧

ONE OF THE MOST IMPORTANT MODELS IN MODERN FINANCE IS THE CAPITAL asset pricing model (CAPM).[1] It is the basis for a number of index models, especially capitalization-weighted indexes like the S&P 500. Many hundreds of billions of dollars are invested in index funds and cap-weighted indexes by individuals and institutions alike. This is a big deal.

ASSESSING THE STRENGTH OF CAPITALIZATION-WEIGHTED INVESTING

For most of us, our biggest bet is in equities. Is this the right bet? To get a handle on that, let's suppose we have a perfect crystal ball. It can't tell us the share prices of every asset in the years ahead, but it can tell us what cash flows we're going to get from every investment we could make, into the future forever. It lets us calculate the true *fair value* of every asset in the market, as the discounted net present value of all of these future cash flows.

If we know what the earnings from a company will be, and we know what interest rate or rates of return we need to justify the risk of holding a stock, then we can assign a fair value to the present price of the stock. In essence, the fair value would be what we are willing to pay to get those future earnings.

If we all know that true fair value, then the market value will match that value. In this world, the capital asset pricing model will be correct, in the sense that there is no way to boost returns without boosting risk. In the parlance of the finance world, this index will be perfectly *mean-variance efficient*.

Now let's suppose our crystal ball is just a little bit cloudy and we can't see the future precisely. Then we can't know what true fair value is. But we can know that every stock, every asset, every bond is going to be trading above or below what its ultimate true fair value is. Even the most ardent fans of the efficient markets hypothesis would say, "That's reasonable. That's reality."

Now if every asset is trading above or below its true fair value, then any index that is capitalization-weighted (price-weighted or valuation-weighted) is automatically going to have us overexposed to every single asset that's trading above its true fair value and underexposed to every single asset that's trading below its true fair value. Far more than half of the index will be invested in the half of the market that's overvalued, for the simple reason that the index weight of an asset is directly related to the size of the pricing error.

This notion of an unknowable true fair value is not mere intellectual game playing. It has some concrete implications for the market. It means that capitalization-weighted indexes, on which the majority of our entire investment portfolios rely, are fundamentally, structurally flawed and will inherently overweight every stock that's above fair value and underweight every stock that's below fair value.

Let's look at what that does to returns. If you put most of your money in assets that are above fair value—and, reciprocally, too little in assets that are below fair value—you get a *return drag*. The cap-weighted indexes are producing returns that are below what they should be or below what they would be in a true-fair-value-weighted portfolio. Importantly, the returns are also below what would be available in a valuation-indifferent index (one that is not based on the valuation of a company, its price to earnings (P/E) ratio, or its book value, for instance).

INVESTING IN EQUAL-WEIGHTED INDEXES: A BETTER ALTERNATIVE

If you construct an index that is valuation indifferent—that doesn't care what the P/E ratios are, and doesn't care what the market capitalization is—then return drag disappears. Even better, you can quantify return. It's about 2 to 4 percent per year. How many managers out there reliably add 2 to 4 percent per year in the very long run? Darn few of them.

This is what can happen in an equal-weighted index, where the same amount of money is put in each stock, no matter what the stock price is. Although it's a seriously flawed index, equal weighting will outperform a cap-weighted index. Many observers think that equal-weighted indexes outperform mainstream capitalization indexes because they have a small-stock bias: Small companies beat large because they have a value bias, and cheap stocks outperform expensive ones. That's not quite correct.

What equal weighting does is to weight the portfolio in a valuation-indifferent fashion: It will underweight every stock that's large, regardless of whether it's cheap or dear, and overweight every stock that's small, regardless of whether it's cheap or dear. How does this compare with the cap-weighted index, where every stock that's overvalued is overweight? In the equal-weighted index it's random luck—50/50. You have even odds of being over- or underweight, whether it's overvalued or undervalued.

Let's look at a concrete example. Suppose we have a world with two groups of stocks, one consisting of all of the overvalued companies, and another consisting of all of the undervalued companies. Each has a true fair value of $100, although the marketplace doesn't know this true fair value. One group of stocks is estimated by the market to really be worth $50, while the other is estimated to really be worth $150, but both valuations are wrong. Capitalization weighting puts 75 percent on that overvalued group of stocks.

Now suppose that over the next ten years, today's errors are corrected. Both portfolios move to $100. However, a new 50 percent error is introduced in each asset, because various news or analyst reports convince investors that some of these companies now look really good and the others look really bad. The portfolio is reallocated into a new overvalued and undervalued component, drawing from some of each of the first two portfolios. The result is a *steady state:* The size of the errors stays steady, but the old errors have been corrected and replaced with new errors.

In this world, the long-run capitalization-weighted return is zero. You gain nothing.

So, how does a valuation-indifferent portfolio help us? Instead of having 75 percent invested in the portfolio of overvalued and 25 percent in the portfolio of undervalued stocks, we have randomized to 50 percent in the overvalued stocks and 50 percent in the under-valued stocks. The former drops 33 percent, the latter doubles. So, the valuation-indifferent portfolio gains the average of these, or 33 percent.[2] The return is 2.8 percent per year, compounded annually. Capitalization weighting has cost us 2.8 percent per year, *even if we have no way of knowing which stocks are over- or undervalued.*

One implication of this world of uncertain true fair value is that we should expect a *size effect;* namely, that large-capitalization stocks should underperform small-capitalization stocks on average, over time. Why? Suppose our crystal ball allows us to see a list of the ten highest true-fair-value companies. What's the likelihood that the highest true-fair-value company will also be the largest-capitalization company? It'll happen from time to time, but it's not likely in any given year. Some less-valuable company will most likely have enough positive error (overvaluation) to eclipse that top-ranked largest-capitalization company. That positive pricing error turns into a return drag, as the market seeks out the company's true fair value.

This means that, most of the time, the largest-capitalization company should underperform the average stock. Does it? Yes!

In the April/May 2005 issue of the *Financial Analysts Journal,* I published a short study in which I looked back over the last eighty years and asked the question, "How often does the number-one-ranked company in market capitalization outperform the average stock over the next one year, three years, five years, and ten years?" The simple answer seems to be that on average, over time, about 80 percent of the time, the largest-capitalization company underperforms over the next ten years. The magnitude of that underperformance is huge: The largest-capitalization company, on average, underperforms the average stock by 40 to 50 percentage points over the next ten years. This is illustrated in Table 8.1.

You'd expect the same pattern but with less reliability in the top-ten companies. What's the likelihood that the ten highest true-fair-

TABLE 8.1

Comparison of Largest-Cap Companies with Market Average

How Often Did Largest-Cap Stock Beat Average?

	After 1 year	After 3 years	After 5 years	After 10 years
1926–2004	38%	30%	25%	24%
Std. deviation	49%	46%	44%	43%
Adjusted *t*-stat.	−2.2	−3.1	−3.0	−2.4
1964–2004	34%	26%	19%	16%
Std. deviation	48%	44%	40%	37%
Adjusted *t*-stat.	−2.1	−2.8	−2.9	−2.6
Subsequent Largest-Cap Return versus Average Stock Return				
1926–2004				
Std. deviation	−7.1%	−15.4%	−24.0%	−39.9%
1964–2004				
Std. deviation	−9.3%	−18.7%	−29.3%	−47.8%

Source: Research Affiliates, LLC

value companies will identically match the ten largest market capitalization companies? Slim to none. Some of the top ten will deserve to be there; their true fair value is huge, as is their market capitalization. Some of them will not deserve to be there. This symmetric pattern of errors will push some companies that don't deserve to be in the top ten of market capitalization, due to an overly optimistic view of the companies' prospects, into that top ten, crowding out some of the companies that deserve to be there, but where their future prospects are underestimated by the market, out of the top ten.

What do we find? On average over time, seven out of ten of the top-ten stocks underperform the average stock over the next ten years, and three out of ten outperform. Meaning three out of ten probably deserved to be in that top ten. The average underperformance is again huge, but less than for the number-one stock: 26 percentage points over the next ten years, as is shown in Table 8.2.

How do we reconcile the fact that capitalization-weighted portfolios are *market clearing*—that is, they span the entire market, and they cover everything in exactly the proportion that the

TABLE 8.2

Comparison of Top-Ten Stocks with Market Average

What Percentage of Top-Ten Stocks Beat Average?

	After 1 year	After 3 years	After 5 years	After 10 years
1926–2004	45%	41%	38%	32%
Std. deviation	27%	26%	25%	25%
Adjusted *t*-stat.	−2.9	−2.8	−3.0	−3.2
1964–2004	40%	37%	32%	29%
Std. deviation	26%	25%	22%	22%
Adjusted *t*-stat.	−5.4	−4.2	−4.8	−3.9

Subsequent Top-Ten Return versus Average Stock Return

	After 1 year	After 3 years	After 5 years	After 10 years
1926–2004	−2.9%	−9.6%	−15.0%	−26.2%
Std. deviation	2.7%	4.7%	7.1%	13.6%
1964–2004	−3.6%	−9.6%	−19.7%	−30.7%
Std. deviation	4.4%	6.0%	8.3%	18.5%

Source: Research Affiliates, LLC

market owns those assets—with a return drag that is so easy to eliminate?

GETTING THE 2 PERCENT OF ALPHA

This gets us back to finance theory, specifically the capital asset pricing model (the CAPM). This model suggests (indeed, subject to a handful of assumptions, proves) that the market-clearing portfolio must be mean-variance efficient. What does that mean in plain English? It means that a portfolio that holds the same assets as the total market, in the same proportions as the total market, cannot be outperformed at lower risk by any other portfolio; it's *the* ideal portfolio. The CAPM also suggests that every asset in the market will have an expected return that can be precisely measured based on the expected return of the market.

If an asset tends to magnify the market movements two-to-one (in the lingo of finance, its *beta* is 2.0), then it will have an expected return exactly twice as high, relative to cash yields as the market's premium over cash yields. Both of these elements of the CAPM are widely accepted, widely used, and demonstrably false.

But the simple fact is, the model works if your market portfolio spans everything: every stock, every bond, every house, every office building, everything you could invest in on the planet, even including *human capital*, which is the net present value of all of our respective labors, going into the future. There's no index like that; it doesn't exist and it never will. You can immediately say that the S&P 500 is not the market, and anyone who says that it's efficient because it *is* the market is missing the point: it's not the market.

The other problem is that the CAPM makes some simplifying assumptions, to make the mathematical proof work:

- All investors are rational.
- All share the same tolerance for risk.
- Investors can borrow and lend at the same risk-free rate—without limit.
- Investors are all indifferent regarding the amount of leverage in our portfolio (million-to-one leverage? No problem!).
- There are no taxes.

There are other assumptions, but these are the main ones. I'm sure our readers will find these assumptions to be entirely reasonable (not!).

Thus, it is easy to see why we can improve on cap weighting. Any index that is replicable, objective, transparent, and focused on large and liquid companies, which are easily traded, is a potentially useful index. Any such index that is valuation-indifferent should beat the capitalization-weighted stock market. If we don't care what P/E ratios are or what the price is when setting how large our investment in an asset should be, we should beat cap weighting in the long run.

What could we do to accomplish this goal? We could find the thousand largest companies by book value, and create an index weighted by book value. In this fashion, we pay no regard to the price or the market capitalization, simply indexing by book value.

We could index based on revenues—which companies have the highest revenue base or sales, and then weight them by revenues or sales. We could even do it based on head count. Which are the thousand biggest employers in the United States? How many people do they employ? Weight the index by the number of employees.

You can do anything of this sort, anything that captures the scale of a company, so you have a bias toward large and liquid companies that is replicable and objective but that doesn't pay attention to valuation. Does it work? Absolutely.

Figure 8.1 shows that the thousand largest by capitalization over the past 43 years (the top bar) would have taken every dollar you invested and turned it into roughly $70. That's what the biggest bull market in U.S. capital markets history, from 1975 to 1999, does for us. But if we use any of these other measures—any of them—we do far better. For the average of these alternative approaches to indexing, we do better than twice as well, with almost $160 for every dollar at starting value. It's a huge gap. Look at what happened after 1999. The S&P 500 is still down 11 percent in total

FIGURE 8.1

Comparison of Indexes, 1962–2004
All Fundamental Indexes, Growth of $1, 1962–2004

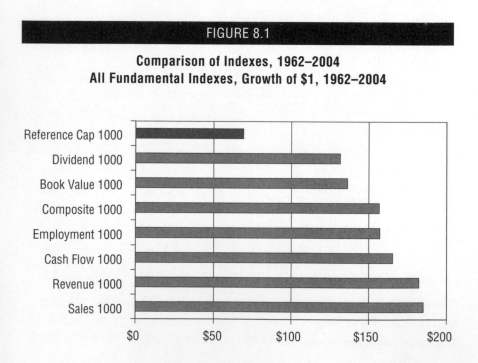

return, including income, after five years. Fundamentally weighted indexes are up 45 percent.

Clearly, fundamental indexing does appear to offer structural advantages over conventional capitalization weighting. How well does it work over time? In Table 8.3 geometric return is the leftmost column. The S&P 500 comes in at 10.53 percent a year over the last 43 years. The *reference cap*—the thousand largest by market capitalization, without the ministrations of the committee that selects which companies make it into the S&P—stands about 0.18 percent lower, at 10.35 percent per annum. This was computed to give us a fair apples-with-apples comparison, thousand-stock indexes weighted in different ways. The average of the fundamental indexes? The worst of the fundamental indexes produces a 12.01 percent annual return, much better than the conventional indexes, while the best produces almost 13 percent. The average is 12.50 percent, fully 2.15 percent ahead of the comparable reference cap portfolio.

The *t*-statistic for the composite, on the far right, is 3.4. These results have well under one chance in a thousand of being *random*

TABLE 8.3

How Significant Is the CAPM Alpha?

	Geometric Return	Excess Return vs. REF CAP	Excess Return *t*-stat	CAPM Alpha vs. REF CAP	Standard Error	*t*-stat for Alpha = 0
S&P 500	10.53%	0.18%	0.76	0.23%	0.23%	1.00
Reference Cap	10.35%	—	—	—	—	—
Book Value	12.11%	1.76%	3.22	1.98%	0.53%	3.71
Cash Flow	12.61%	2.26%	3.72	2.51%	0.60%	4.21
Revenue	12.87%	2.52%	3.25	2.57%	0.78%	3.32
Sales	12.91%	2.56%	3.36	2.63%	0.76%	3.46
Gross Dividends	12.01%	1.66%	2.02	2.39%	0.75%	3.17
Employment	12.48%	2.13%	2.98	2.15%	0.72%	3.00
Composite	**12.47%**	**2.12%**	**3.26**	**2.44%**	**0.63%**	**3.87**
Average, Excl Comp	**12.50%**	**2.15%**	**3.09**	**2.37%**	**0.70%**	**3.41**

Source: Research Affiliates, LLC

luck. If we risk adjust, taking account of the fact that most of these fundamental indexes are less risky than the capitalization-weighted indexes, we are adding closer to 2.5 percent per annum on a risk-adjusted basis. You aren't committing so much to the popular high fliers, the Krispy Kremes of the world, and then watching them implode. The statistical significance of the risk-adjusted returns is off the charts—nearly a 4.0 *t*-statistic.

How consistent is this approach? During economic expansions, you add almost 2 percent a year. During recessions—when you most need those returns—we can add 3.5 percent. During bull markets, this approach adds 40 basis points. We add less in bull markets, because they are often driven as much by psychology than by the underlying fundamental realities of the companies. But, unlike value investors, we can at least keep pace during bull markets adding modest value along the way. During bear markets, this approach adds 600 to 700 basis points per annum. Bear markets are when reality sets in and people say, "Show me the numbers." Finally, during periods of rising rates, 2.5 percent is added. During periods of falling rates, 1.5 percent is added (see Table 8.4).

TABLE 8.4

Results in Expansion and Recession, Bull and Bear Markets, Rising and Falling Rates

Market & Economic Environment	Expansion	Recession	Bull Market	Bear Market	Rising Rates	Falling Rates
S&P 500	11.75%	3.15%	20.81%	−24.02%	18.05%	5.08%
Reference Cap	11.66%	2.46%	20.89%	−24.89%	18.13%	4.73%
Book Value	13.19%	5.51%	21.20%	−19.30%	19.81%	6.53%
Cash Flow	13.60%	6.55%	21.63%	−18.62%	20.94%	6.61%
Revenue	13.82%	7.03%	22.24%	−19.36%	20.99%	7.00%
Sales	13.84%	7.24%	22.27%	−19.30%	21.02%	7.06%
Gross Dividends	12.70%	7.74%	19.68%	−15.27%	20.38%	5.99%
Employment	13.63%	5.49%	21.62%	−19.08%	20.87%	6.44%
Composite	13.40%	6.77%	21.26%	−18.09%	20.56%	6.63%

Source: Research Affiliates, LLC

CONCLUSION

In short, we find that fundamental indexing works especially well in an environment of recession or a bear market or rising rates. But it also adds modest value in the more benign environments, with economic expansion, falling interest rates, and a bull market in stocks. Value investing generally does not add value during expansions, bull markets, or periods of rising rates.

Is it an index? Of course it can be an index. Is it passive? Yes: It's replicable, formulaic, transparent, and objectively constructed. Is it a total market portfolio? Not in a capital asset pricing model context, because it doesn't span all marketable assets equivalent to their weight in the actual market. But, as we've already observed, no index fits this criterion.

Are the cap-weighted indexes efficient? That is to say, can you improve on them by constructing better indexes, without taking on more risk? Yes, you can, so the cap-weighted indexes are not efficient. The classic indexes are not the market, and no commercially viable market portfolio exists; and even if one did it wouldn't matter, because the capital-asset pricing model is predicated on so many structurally flawed assumptions that the notion that the cap-weighted indexes must be efficient is the same as the notion that the underlying assumptions must be true.

Finally, there are very real implications in this model for long-short investing. I suspect that large institutions and pension plans will eventually move large portions of their equity assets into indexes like this. What's a 2 percent difference worth? Let's assume that, with your current portfolio, in 36 years you end up with $1 billion. If you can increase portfolio performance by just 2 percent, you will end up with $2 billion. A 2 percent alpha doubles your cumulative assets over these longer time horizons of pensions.

If you are an individual, the same principle applies. Over 36 years, that 2 percent will double your return. And that's a big number in anybody's book.

CHAPTER 9

The Outsider Trading Scandal

⁓

The official bio of George Gilder is a tad intimidating. He is editor of the Gilder Technology Report, *chairman of Gilder Publishing, LLC, and a senior fellow of the Discovery Institute.*

Gilder attended Exeter Academy and Harvard University, studying under and working with Henry Kissinger. He co-authored The Party That Lost Its Head *and served as a speechwriter for Nelson Rockefeller, George Romney, and Richard Nixon. In the 1970s, Gilder began an excursion into the causes of poverty, which resulted in his books* Men and Marriage *(1972);* Visible Man *(1978); and* Wealth and Poverty *(1981).* Wealth and Poverty *was a seminal book for the conservative movement and was an intellectual source for much of the Reagan Revolution.*

Gilder pioneered the formulation of supply-side economics. His investigation into wealth creation led to a deeper examination of the lives of entrepreneurs, culminating in The Spirit of Enterprise *(1986) and his best-selling work,* Microcosm *(1989). A subsequent book,* Life After Television, *was a prophecy of the future of computers and telecommunications and a prelude to his book on the future of telecommunications,* Telecosm *(2000).*

George's latest book is The Silicon Eye *(2005), a fascinating narrative of personality and technology in which Gilder shares his inside knowledge of Silicon Valley and illustrates how the unpredictable mix of genius, drive, and luck can turn a startup into a Fortune 500 company.*

George lives with his wife, Nini, and has four children. He is a runner and cross-country skier. (I remember him once passing the horse-drawn sleigh I was riding in—a moment that inspired me to get my derriere in gear and start exercising.) And he is one heck of a nice guy, a great bon vivant and wonderful storyteller. Here, George tells us to "ignore the outside noise and focus on acquiring real fundamental knowledge."   —John Mauldin

The Outsider Trading Scandal

by George Gilder

∽

VALUE VERSUS VANITY. DAY-TRADING VERSUS BUY-AND-HOLD. EFFICIENT MAR-
kets versus random walk. Growth versus value. Momentum versus
discounted cash flow. Buffett versus Lynch. Graham and Dodd versus Aswath Damodaran or Mary Meeker. Technical analysis versus
technology paradigms. Risk-enhanced riches versus gambler's ruin.
The beat goes on, and the battle never ends until the fat-laden gurus gag, and the investors' money runs out.

Ruffling the waves on a *Forbes* investment cruise in the Baltic in
mid-2005 was a pungent debate on these contentious issues of personal investment. Technical Titan Ralph Bloch cited his own annual
42 percent gains and sneered at bubble-era fundamentalists such as
Meeker and Henry Blodget and current technology writers such as
myself and Nanotech guru Josh Wolfe. Bloch and fellow technician
Jim Stack made a powerful case that the best and most objective
guidance to the future movement of the markets comes from the
market itself. Regularly making similar arguments are the *Investor's
Business Daily*, *Barron's*, and scores of investment newsletters.

It seems like a plausible idea. Watch the movements of the market and interpret their significance. No other source of information
can yield so objective a view of securities as the changes in the
prices themselves. Reflecting all the knowledge available in the
market and all the decisions to buy and sell, the patterns of change
in market prices offer empirical scientific data. By comparison, the
information divulged by companies and experts is skewed by bias,
subjectivity, self-interest, and murky interpretation.

Only rarely does anyone point out that without fundamentals—without close and necessarily subjective scrutiny of the

actual performance and potential of each company—markets would contain virtually no information at all. Markets would slouch through the kind of random walk that Burton Malkiel and others have famously described. In a random world, luck would dominate skill. Like casinos or lotteries, markets would fall to the inexorable law of gambler's ruin.

THE VALUE OF INFORMATION

To avoid this grim fate, what is the one thing that investors should know as they engage in buying and selling securities? They should know that an economy is not a casino or a lottery. Nor is it a physical or material system. It is an arena of information. It is governed by mathematical laws of information similar to the laws that determine the capacity of telephone lines and wireless spectrum—the same laws of information that shape biological change through the genetic code or shepherd calls through your code division multiple access (CDMA) digital cell phone. In markets, the winners are the people with the best information, mostly inside information.

The key insight of *information theory* is that information is measured by the degree to which it is unexpected. Information is "news," gauged by its *surprisal*, technically called *entropy*. A stream of predictable bits conveys no information at all. A stream of chaotic noise conveys no information. To convey a high-entropy message—lots of information—takes a low-entropy carrier, a predictable vessel, that allows the receiver to distinguish the message from the noise.

Why do you care? Entropy, the technical word for news value, is at the heart of markets and making money. Entropy is the source of profit. The predictable returns are already incorporated in the price, which in the end will settle to the risk-adjusted return on capital, or the interest rate plus a risk premium.

Technical analysts parade their market models down the runways in undulating patterns: comely regularities and curvaceous symmetries. What's not to like? A popular school of analysis celebrates the market as a fractal, evincing the fashionable swirls and whorls and "strange attractors" of chaos theory. In the last year, Benoit Mandelbrot has published his *Misbehavior of Markets* and Phillip Ball *Critical Mass* to show that the laws of fractals and physics capture the deep reality of markets.

What does information theory tell you about such ideas? Stanford University's Thomas Cover, the leading information theorist of the day, put Mandelbrot's set—the colorful whorls of intricate design and apparent complexity of Mandelbrot's fractal display—on the jacket of his canonical book *Elements of Information Theory*. Graphic artists often use the Mandelbrot set as an epitome of dense information.

But information theory itself is full of surprises. Inside the jacket of his book, Cover writes, "The information content of the fractal on the cover is essentially *zero*." Nada. Complexity is measured by the number of lines in the computer code needed to produce the effect. The product of a simple computer algorithm, Mandlebrot's fractal bears virtually no content at all according to this measure of information theory. It is all froth on a core of simple algebra.

In a 2005 book, *A Different Universe*, Nobel Laureate physicist Robert Loughlin of Stanford describes such studies of froth as "baubles" and "supremely unimportant." It is like analyzing water by focusing on the bubbles as it boils, a phase change phenomenon still not understood and full of chaotic enigmas. Such frothy data analysis epitomizes spurious science. It focuses on trivial patterns yielding small or chaotic effects that are divorced from the actual substance of causes and consequences.

In a similar way, information theory dismisses the many books that attempt to reduce markets to material laws. The legendary information theorist Gregory Chaitin demonstrates that the laws of physics, measured by the same gauge of algorithmic complexity, bear far less information than do social phenomena such as people, companies, and markets. To predict the markets by physical law is like predicting the outcome of the Super Bowl by studying the laws of football.

Markets are living things fraught with all the complexity and information of life. The essence of life is that it is governed by information that is separate from its substrate. Just as computer information can be put on any kind of regular carrier, from a piece of paper to a grain of sand, information is not intrinsically chemical or physical. As MIT's Norbert Wiener explained: "Information is information, not matter or energy. No materialism that does not admit this can survive in the present day." As Wiener put it, "The brain does not secrete thought as the liver does bile."

As manifestations of the interplay of human minds, markets are analogous to biological phenomena. Although the analogy is not exact, it conveys a deep truth. The controlling knowledge of economics and biology both reside deep inside the nuclei of cells and companies.

In biology, this order of things is termed the *Central Dogma*, as framed by Nobel Laureate Francis Crick who with James Watson first defined the structure of DNA. The Central Dogma ordains that DNA comes first and programs the proteins. DNA is a predictable carrier that can bear any possible sequence of coded nucleotides. The content is entirely separate from the contents. That is why DNA could carry the genetic information of all the living creatures that have ever existed or presumably will exist.

Because there are 64 DNA codons and an alphabet of only 20 amino acids, biological information has to flow from the more potent information source (the DNA with its 64 possible symbols) to the less potent one (the amino acid proteins with just 20 symbols). Lamarck and his follower Lysenko were wrong. You cannot change the DNA program by altering the arrangement of physical proteins. You cannot create a *new Soviet man* by changing his environment.

In economics, the analogous principle—the central dogma—is that the concept precedes the concrete. The design precedes the product. The plan precedes the company. You cannot predict the future of markets or companies by examining the fractal patterns of their previous price movements.

The contrary temptation has persisted throughout history. People have relentlessly tried to read the mind of God or the destiny of men and nations and companies in patterns in the sands or the stars. But you cannot fathom the DNA by contemplating the shape of people's heads (phrenology) or reading the lines on their hands (palmistry) or examining the constellations at the moment of their birth (astrology). Similarly, you cannot predict future movements of markets by weighing the current patterns of stock prices. There simply is not enough information in current prices to reveal future prices.

Outsiders doing technical analysis can occasionally be effective, particularly when guided and seasoned by an intuitive or stealthy mastery of fundamentals. But technical analysis is essentially parasitic. It is *outside* information. For its validity, it depends on the fundamental judgments of insiders and the insights of knowledgeable analysts who appraise the DNA of companies: their management, their financial data, and their technological endowments.

Ultimately ruling markets are the real facts of supply and demand, the realities of finance, and the intricate details of technology paradigms and execution. But the outside temptation persists. The conventional wisdom, once again invoked on the *Forbes* cruise, is that stock markets ride on toxic tides of greed and fear and can be best appraised through technical indices of their movements. Through the long history chronicled by Charles Mackay in *Extraordinary Delusions and the Madness of Crowds*, shares have all too often behaved like chaotic fractals, soaring wildly up on mad swirls of ignorant momentum and then plummeting down in dire spirals of panic. From the Tulipmania of the seventeenth century to the plunge of 1987 and the technology depression of 2000, chaos and volatility have all too often ruled.

The promise of the Internet is *infocopia:* the instant spread of detailed information. Largely fulfilled, this promise brings the world more instantaneous information on more companies and securities than ever before. So why in the midst of an information age, when capital and data zip around the planet at the speed of light, do markets still behave like tulip auctions in 1690, when high-speed data traveled by carrier pigeons?

THE DEARTH OF INSIDE INFORMATION

A key reason is the *outsider trading scandal.* The law for information disclosure by public companies and aspirant public companies prohibits the release of materially significant news unless it is published simultaneously to the world. This well-meaning rule is supposed to create a level playing field where no investors have the advantage of inside knowledge. But a level playing field means no information, which is defined as a deformation of the level. Information, like life, is disequilibrium. What the SEC accomplishes is to reduce the amount of real information in stock prices.

Less information means increased volatility and more vulnerability to outside events. With the entire field of information about companies a regulated arena, information does not bubble up from firms spontaneously in raw and ambiguous form with executives and engineers freely expressing their views and even investing on the basis of them. It emerges as various forms of processed public relations.

Intended to prevent fraud and illegal insider trading, this rule does not prevent criminals from manipulating markets. Criminals, by definition, observe the law only to break it more ingeniously. The idea of stopping them by reducing information for everyone else is like stopping terrorists by making everyone else lie at airports about the complete control of their luggage. It makes the regulator feel he is doing something, but it does not affect the criminal.

What the regulation of material information accomplishes instead is to sharply inhibit the flow of inside news from companies. Inside information—the flow of intimate detail about the progress of technologies and product tests and research and development and diurnal sales data—is in fact the only force that makes any long-term difference in stock performance. Yet it is precisely this information that is denied to public investors. Information about technology cannot filter out day by day from different inside sources to knowledgeable people who might grasp the significance of it. Instead, information is parceled out by departments of public affairs under guidance of lawyers. The resulting press releases are mostly bombast and bafflegab, zero-entropy documents teetering over a bay of safe-harbor statements often larger than the release itself.

Entrepreneurial information from deep inside companies, not from the investment counsel or PR firm, is the chief real knowledge in the economy. Acquiring and comprehending it is the chief work of inside entrepreneurs. Such knowledge is by no means self-evident; insiders often get it wrong. But nothing else is of much value at all. By excluding inside news from influencing the day-to-day movements of prices, the United States effectively blinds its stock markets

As a result, the pullulating mass of data and news about technology companies is constipated into a few synthetic disclosure events. What should be a steady outpouring of knowledge—some of it hype, some confusing, most of it ambiguous, like business life itself—emerges instead as a series of media events that leave out everything interesting. Pivotal are quarterly financial reports and merger and acquisition announcements.

Concentrated rather than diffused, such information takes the form of discrete nuggets and events—P&L or M&A—that are more subject to theft and manipulation. Thus, the government's control of information creates more binary moments of disclosure and more opportunities for inside trading. Moreover, because only acquiring companies can know all the intimate inside details about companies they are purchasing, mergers and acquisitions become the decisive moments of value recognition. Anticipating them becomes a major preoccupation of analysts.

With inside information banished from public markets, privateers capture the wealth. The flow of capital gains bifurcates to the residual inside traders who are legally permitted to learn the intimate facts of the companies in which they invest. Huge winners are conglomerateurs such as Warren Buffett of Berkshire Hathaway and Jeffrey Immelt of General Electric and venture capitalists such as Donald Valentine of Sequoia and John Doerr of Kleiner Perkins Caulfield and Byers.

GE and Berkshire Hathaway are not companies at all, but portfolios of diverse assets. Their strength is full access to inside knowledge about their holdings and potential purchases. Similarly, venture capitalists command full intimate knowledge of their target firms. When Google went public at $87 per share, most of the returns went to venture partnerships such as Kleiner that bought the shares for 40 cents.

The irony is that when the company went public, its information went private. As it plunged into the enforced secrecy of *fair disclosure* regulations, Google drastically reduced the flow of information to its shareholders. The public is left largely in the dark, learning little about their holdings outside of quarterly announcements, occasional press releases, and personality profiles in business magazines.

Such markets are vulnerable to outside information—the outsider trading scandal. Mostly working in the dark, investors become paranoid and jump at every movement in the shadows. They debate the implicit punctuation in speeches by Alan Greenspan. They gauge the relative milligrams in the weight of merger rumors. They even speculate on what will be the next company deemed to hold an "ascendant technology" by the *Gilder Technology Report*. They contemplate technical charts and invest on the basis of momentum, by definition ignorant.

In their ignorance, investors become manic-depressive. They become prey to pundits and politicians who may know even less than they do, but who command the media.

THE FALLACY OF IMBALANCE FEARS

During a trade tussle with China in the midst of the first decade of the new century, the U.S. Secretary of the Treasury John Snow chose to expound his economic wisdom in a prominent article on the op-ed page of the *Wall Street Journal* (May 26, 2005). As the former railroad executive saw it, the world economic system faced a dire crisis of imbalance. In his thousand-word essay, he used the word *imbalance*, inflected with rhetorical frowns, no fewer than twelve times.

By paying this almost liturgical tribute to the virtues of equilibrium in international economics, Snow invoked the single most pervasive fallacy in the minds of investors and their guides and gurus: the idea that economies should be *balanced* or are naturally balanced at their borders. Following from this insight is the notion that imbalances must be rectified. If they persist, they portend a catastrophic "Day of Reckoning," as Benjamin Friedman of Harvard put it in a famous text.

Such litanies of equilibrium economics annually agitate the Economic Summit in Davos, Switzerland, and lugubriate in the worldly wisdom of such sages as Buffett and Gates who believe that the U.S. economy is insightfully depicted as *Squanderville* because foreigners prefer its assets to its goods. From all parts of the political spectrum, tomes pile up in an Amazonian delta, invoking with biblical resonance a "Great Reckoning" (James Dale Davidson), or "Great Unravelling" (Paul Krugman of Princeton), or "Financial Reckoning Day" (William Bonner), or "Coming Collapse" (James Turk) or "Coming Crash" (John Talbot), capped off with several prophetic schools of "Coming Depression": "Inflationary" (Ravi Batra), "Deflationary" (Robert Prechter), and just "Great" (Doug Casey).

In the absence of real inside information, such outside noise can carry the day. Snow did not divulge just what imbalances were upsetting him. Was the problem that for more than a decade China and the United States have been growing far faster than the rest of the world? Snow did express the idea that Europe and Japan were not growing fast enough. He also deplored, by innuendo, the trade gap, which has persisted for a hundred years or so while the United States came to dominate the world economy.

Perhaps the basic problem is that U.S. companies collectively command close to half of the market capitalization of the world's publicly traded corporations and that the United States produces close to 30 percent of global gross domestic product (GDP) with just 5 percent of the world's population. Growing since the early 1980s, these skews of wealth and growth favoring the United States understandably evoke envy and distress among many of the suave continental equilibrists at Davos. But only Snow knows why they should concern U.S. investors, or why we should blame China for its immensely fruitful tie to the dollar that creates a dollar zone in which both countries flourish.

The imbalances concern U.S. investors chiefly because they concern Snow, and artificial crises mean more government intervention in global markets by ignorant politicians who think the Chinese are manipulating their currency price by tying it to the dollar. With a trade balance the most unlikely possible configuration of capital and goods movements, concern about a trade gap means constant government intervention in the global economy and lower stock prices everywhere.

With market prices moving by multiples on the basis of political noise from the likes of Snow, investors spend most of their time in a hair trigger trance. When the Fed makes a mistake on interest rates or the government makes another blunder on broadband policy or immigration rules or tax rates, the markets overreact. Volatility is an effect of the very ignorance that the new information tools are designed to overcome.

Even on the World Wide Web, blinded pundits cover blinded markets. With inquiring analysts barred from any "material" information not divulged at once to the world, reporters focus on the personalities of executives and on financial data, necessarily retrospective and thus irrelevant to future prices. Business magazines, for example, must check all facts with the companies. Because of information disclosure laws, all data must be closely held until it is officially announced. No facts can be revealed or verified until they are fully understood by the firms' executives and deemed safe to be divulged without risk of future embarrassment. Such news is obsolete by the time it is announced. With an *omerta* on the companies themselves and paralysis of insiders around them, the markets fill up with misinformation, momentum, and so-called "technical" twaddle about the market itself.

In mid-July 2005, analysts discounted PowerOne's (PWER) assertion that it had twenty customers for its key product. In fact, they estimated the correct number was forty customers, but CEO Steve Goldman could not divulge such new information until it was thoroughly vetted by the company lawyers for unveiling to the world. By that time, the number will in all likelihood have changed again.

Because of such distortions amplified and propagated through the markets, the huge expansion of financial coverage on the Internet has not resulted in more rational and informed pricing of stocks. In an information economy, inside information is the basis of share value. It is the DNA that ultimately shapes the behavior of companies. Yet such inside information is barred as much as possible from the markets.

The essence of SEC rules is "don't invest in anything you know about." The chief message of many state governments is to invest in the state lottery, where no one knows more than you do. The safest stock market investment is an index fund that bears no information at all. Executives at companies avoid insider rules by putting their own purchases and sales of stock on an automated program. This may protect the executives from litigation, but it also protects the public from the information that insider activity might otherwise impart. Prices contain less information, making the market a more perilous arena.

As Richard Vigilante and Andy Readleaf of Whitebox Strategies put it in their forthcoming book, *Minds and Markets:* "In pursuit of fairness, the SEC is trying to create a market in which all available information circulates perfectly." Perfect competition is the implicit ideal. "No doubt they would prefer this to be a market of perfect information (which is impossible). But since they can't do that, they are creating a market of scarce information, in which the job of resolving uncertainty contains a much greater share of luck than of judgment. It's the replacement of judgment with guessing, entrepreneurship with luck, that is the general problem of which technical trading is only an instance."

To realize the benefit of the World Wide Web on those information markets that focus on stocks, the current rules on the disclosure of material information should be rescinded. At a minimum, they are in clear violation of the first amendment. Fraudulent manipulation of shares will remain a criminal act and can be prosecuted without at the same time regulating and stultifying the entire flow of information from companies.

Information wants to be free and the more of it incorporated in the prices of shares the more robust will be the market and the less subject to manipulation, euphoria, and panic. Through the Internet, stock exchanges can escape the popular Keynesian characterization as a casino and fulfill still better their real role in the intelligent investment of capital. Greed and fear can only give way to knowledge if knowledge is legal.

THE INVESTOR'S CHALLENGE

The key rule for investors is to ignore the outside noise and focus on acquiring real, fundamental knowledge about companies. The fundamentals will ultimately prevail. DNA will trump the manifestations of matter. Cryptically coiled in the nuclei of companies, inside knowledge is harder to get under the new regime. But it remains irrepressible.

The Internet is full of sources of competitive analysis and technological expertise. New companies are emerging with powerful ways of obtaining and revealing the crucial troves of inside knowledge that determine the destiny of companies. Some of this information is being made available to the public by vendors such as Gerson-Lehrman with software that enables quick links from investors to hundreds of thousands of available experts. A new generation of information companies, focused on the real sources of value in markets, is creating a new topology of information amid the leveled playing fields of government-enforced ignorance. Watch for these developments and take heed. Skill and information are your remedies for the dismal economics of gamblers' ruin.

CHAPTER 10

The Winner's Rule

⤸

I have known Michael Masterson for more than 20 years. He has one of the smartest business minds I know. Michael has developed a loyal following to his writings in Early to Rise *(www.earlytorise.com), an e-newsletter that mentors more than 400,000 readers. He has been making money for himself and for others for almost two decades. In that time, he's taken only two breaks—each time for two years. The first was after a stint with the Peace Corps, where he came to appreciate relative values and the joy of teaching. The second came at age 39, when he retired from the $100-million-plus business that he and his partner had built over the course of a remarkably successful business career. Michael has been involved in the development of dozens of successful businesses, including two that grew beyond $100 million. And he is the author of the best-selling book* Automatic Wealth *(which I highly recommend for entrepreneurs of all ages). I know, personally, that Michael practices what he preaches. And we should all pay attention when he preaches.* —John Mauldin

⤸

The Winner's Rule

by Michael Masterson

IT'S A TOUGH QUESTION: IF YOU COULD GIVE ONLY ONE PIECE OF ADVICE TO a loved one about the world of wealth, what would it be?

Since I write about wealth building almost every day, worthy candidates spring to mind:

- **Business doesn't happen until you make the first sale.** When I first heard this oft-quoted business adage, I found it absurd. There are so many things to do before a sale can be made, I thought, like setting up an office and installing telephones—not to mention getting the product ready. Later, after I had participated in the stillbirth of dozens of businesses that never had a chance of working in the first place, I realized the wisdom of this axiom. Buying office furniture and printing cards doesn't make the business go. Selling product does. Yes, there are some preparations you need to make before the first sale can be made, but until you have that first check in hand, all you are really doing is spending money.
- **The single most effective way of entering a new market is to offer a popular product at a drastically reduced price.** This was another lesson I bridled against, yet it proved equally important in my business career. In every industry, there is a good market for specialty and high-quality product producers—but capturing a reasonable share of those niche market segments takes lots of money, time, and experience. When you are starting a new business, you are usually short in these three essentials. That's why it's better to resist the allure of high-priced, prestige products in favor of getting at the big market

and selling the most desired products and services at ludicrously cheap prices. It's not always easy to figure out how to undersell the giants, but if you can you will be in a very happy starting place.

- **It's ultimately about selling.** Conventional business wisdom says you make money when you buy, not when you sell. I disagree. Although it helps to buy your product properly, it doesn't take a genius to do that. Anybody with a modicum of common sense can figure out where the market is and haggle for the right price. Great businesspeople make their fortunes by increasing the perceived value of their products, thus ramping up prices and drastically increasing profit margins. (Think Chanel, Rolex, Range Rover.)

- **When choosing a business, select one that can be grown without your personal involvement.** Most professionals, no matter how much they get paid, are wage slaves. And many closely held businesses—especially those built around the personality or drive of a single person—depend for their growth on the commitment of the founder. Avoid getting yourself into this type of business. It flatters the ego but drastically limits your growth potential. In growing your business, make sure it can expand with the addition of more money, property, or people— but not more of you.

- **Before you invest in anything, know exactly how much you are willing to lose—and get out if you hit that stop-loss point.** We begin new ventures with optimism. That's exactly why we need to plan for the worst. With every business venture you invest in, figure out beforehand how you can get out if things fall apart. And make sure you can afford your exit plan. In stock investing, this is easy enough to do by setting a stop-loss point. With other forms of investing—real estate, limited partnerships, and entrepreneurial ventures, for example—it will require more thoughtful planning. Do the planning and stick with it.

- **First, improve your strengths. Then, eliminate your weaknesses.** Generally speaking, you will achieve more in business by learning to do better what you already do well rather than by correcting your weaknesses. If you are a successful real estate broker who is really good at sales presentations but weak on contracts, don't worry so much about getting better at contracts. If necessary, hire someone to handle that part of your business. Spend your self-improvement time advancing from being "really good" to "really great" at sales presentations. This is not to say you should ignore your weaknesses. We should all strive to eliminate those. But you will find that you'll have more success by attending first to your strengths.

- **Focused effort is more effective than a diversified approach to business building.** Ambitious people tend to fall into two groups: those who focus almost entirely on one project at a time and those who prefer to spread themselves out on many projects. The focused approach allows you to acquire mastery faster. The diversified approach gives you more balance. In my career, I've done both. And I have to say that although I'm naturally inclined toward diversification, I've had the most success and made the most money from the focused work. I believe there is a good reason for that. Success in business comes after you have learned the secrets of the industry you are in. That learning process takes time—four or five thousand hours is the norm. If your attention span is limited and you find yourself jumping too quickly to that other lawn (where the grass seems greener), you'll find yourself with too many challenges that you are simply not experienced enough to overcome. If you find that your tendency in business is to skip from one exciting thing to another, train yourself to conquer one field before you step foot in another.

- **Let your winners run and cut your losses short.** Despite what you may have gleaned about success from listening to entertainers and watching movies, most business ideas or ventures that start out poorly fail. This is a very important lesson to learn. It's very easy to get emotionally attached to projects/investments we believe in. That's why it's so important to follow this rule. When the marketplace tells you that your great idea is a loser, don't keep pushing. Close the project and minimize your losses. If you really have a good idea, it will come back to you in the future in another, perhaps better, set of clothing.

- **Pareto's Principle (the 80-20 Rule): 80 percent of your success comes from 20 percent of your resources.** This is perhaps the best-known and most useful axiom of success. Most of the success/income/satisfaction you will get in your career will come from a small portion of your skills/projects/efforts. Make it a regular habit to periodically ask yourself, "Where am I getting most of the benefit here?" and comparing that to where you are putting in the most work.

There may be a few secrets I've forgotten, but these would certainly be on my list of "the most important things I'd like to teach my children about business." But if I had only one secret to teach?

THAT ONE MOST IMPORTANT THING

I have three boys. My oldest son is a computer engineer in the movie industry. My second son is a composer of music. And number three, still in high school, doesn't yet know what he wants to do.

Is there a single "secret of success" that might be helpful to all three of them, given that they have different interests, hopes, and expectations?

The answer isn't obvious. Like any parent, I want them to be happy. But there is something else I want—something I've come to understand now that they are getting out in the world and conducting their own affairs: I want them to be good. I want them to have good manners, to treat other people kindly, to be considerate of those who are less fortunate, and so on.

When they were youngsters, I wanted them to be good too, but for pragmatic reasons. I wanted them to behave themselves in the back of the car so I could drive in peace. I wanted them to stay away from the railroad tracks so they wouldn't get killed. And I wanted them to complete their homework assignments so they could learn.

Now I want them to be good for altruistic reasons. I want them to be able to do what my parents wanted me to do: Leave the world a little better than I found it. Or better yet, to make their world a little better because they are in it. This is not, I'm sure, an unusual notion. Most parents must feel this way.

So that's what I want—that my children accomplish their goals without sacrificing their fun, and become successful without compromising their integrity. I want them to be both good at what they do and good in doing it. Is there something I can tell them that will help them do both?

I think there is. It's a way of conducting yourself in business (and other areas of your life) that can give you success, peace of mind, and happiness. Best of all, perhaps, once learned, it is astonishingly easy to practice.

That secret is this: *In every relationship you get into—every business, social, or personal transaction—make sure that the other person gets as much benefit from it as you do. When considering your own advantages and disadvantages in taking any course of action, consider those of everyone else involved.*

I realize this idea flies in the face of some thinking. It certainly contradicts the way many prominent corporate executives have been behaving lately. Today, the dominant idea of success might be classified as some version of "Looking Out for Number One."

I've tried that approach, I'm embarrassed to say. In my early years as a marketer, I sold products I wasn't proud of at prices I couldn't justify. I rationalized it all by telling myself that I was taking care of my family. That approach didn't work for the long-term success of the business, and it didn't work with regard to the way I felt about myself.

When I took the initiative to do things right, everything turned out better. Business grew. Relationships developed. And my sense of personal satisfaction skyrocketed.

I realized that by making my efforts good for everyone else, my eventual success was all but guaranteed. When people begin to see you as someone they benefit from, they are inclined to bring you more and better deals.

Often, focusing on the other person's interests means taking a risk—taking the chance that the time and money you invest in him will pay off. To some businesspeople, giving before you get is a foolish idea. For me, it's been the source of all my best and most enjoyed accomplishments.

Let me give you an example of how a colleague of mine put this principle to work. About 10 years ago, he decided he wanted to take over a failing periodical business in England. Instead of doing the "smart" thing—putting the squeeze on the business until it was a breath away from death and then stealing it for pennies on the dollar—he voluntarily moved himself and his family to London for six months to nurse the business back to health. He did this based on nothing more than an oral agreement that if he succeeded in doing that, they would then sell him half of the business at some "fair" price.

At that point in my career, I was already an advocate of win-win deals, but it seemed to me that this was taking the good-spirited concept to a new level. By fixing the business before he bought it, my colleague was dramatically raising the price he would have to pay for it. He was doing so without compensation. And by doing it all on an oral contract, he was leaving himself open to being double-crossed.

What happened was very much a happy ending. His new partners got a very nice paycheck for a business they knew was on the verge of bankruptcy. And they returned the favor a few years later when he bought out the rest of the shares by agreeing to the buy-out and not haggling over the price.

Today, that business is one of his most productive assets. Just as importantly, he has great relationships with hundreds of people—employees, vendors, and colleagues—who saw how he behaved and subsequently felt good about doing business with him.

BECOMING AN INVALUABLE EMPLOYEE

If my eldest son were to apply this rule—to think about the interests of the other person/people in the relationship first and yours second—to his current job, he would make sure that the value he is giving his business, as an employee, is worth a good deal more than the cost of his employment (the salary and benefits he is earning).

In my book *Automatic Wealth*, I talk a good deal about how to become an "invaluable" employee. Here is a short list of what my son would do to achieve that status within his company:

- Be among the first to arrive every morning.
- Understand the most important secrets of the business, including how sales are made, how customers are retained, and how new products are created.
- In his spare time, develop skills to help the company achieve its most important goals: growth, profitability, and good customer service.
- Find ways to make his boss more successful.
- Ignore company politics and focus on worthy company goals.

Employees who quickly "get" the core purpose of their business and focus their time and energies on helping the business achieve that goal will be recognized as potential superstars. Such employees will be rewarded, not only with significantly higher financial remuneration but also with greater responsibility and direct access to the people who can advance their futures.

But in explaining all this to my son, I'd make this point very clear: Although you'll get the best rewards for making yourself invaluable to your employer, you won't be invaluable if you do what you do in order to get those rewards. That's the catch. To get the benefits of putting your business partners first, you must really put them first.

BEING AN EFFECTIVE MENTOR

Here's another example of the way this rule works—this time from the management side.

At least half of the success I've enjoyed in business has come from riding on the coattails of young men and women who have worked for me. If I were to take a look at the checks that flow into my consulting practice every month, many more than half of them are signed by individuals who were, at one time, my protégés.

If I've had extraordinary success in mentoring people—and I think I have—it has happened because I never sought to get anything out of my mentorship other than the pleasure of seeing those people succeed. I know that sounds like the most deplorable sort of chest pounding, but I do believe it's true. I have always enjoyed teaching what I've learned to others—and that included showing bright, young employees exactly how I was able to achieve certain things.

By imitating my successes and avoiding my mistakes, they all had faster (and in some cases steeper) ascents in their careers. In many of those cases, I retained business relationships with them—relationships that have proven both very lucrative and personally rewarding.

If my goal had been to use those people to take care of me, I believe they would have sensed it. As a result, I wouldn't be enjoying the close connections and loyalty that I have today.

NICE GUYS FINISH BEST

In an airport bookstore yesterday, I picked up a copy of *Winners Never Cheat* by Jon M. Huntsman. Doubting the premise of the book from the outset ("A self-made billionaire speaks out on honesty and generosity"), I read it with a good degree of skepticism. Here was the owner of one of the largest privately held businesses in the world bragging about how ethical he is. I wondered what some of his former employees and business associates would have to say about his integrity.

It reminded me of a presentation I made a year ago to a group of extremely successful businessmen. My topic was "How to Succeed in Business Without Losing Your Soul." I talked frankly about some of the ethical compromises I'd made in my career, how guilty I'd felt about them, and how it left me wondering if I could have done as well by doing things right.

With one exception, they were unanimous in being shocked and even appalled by what I said. Of course, you can succeed without compromise! Each of them had done it. None of them had ever cheated a little, lied a bit, treated someone a tad unfairly. They were, by their own accounts, angels of virtue who had spent their careers making the world a better place.

A few of these holy men, I discovered later, had worked for such eminently laudable companies as WorldCom, Tyco, and Enron.

Only one of those listening to my confession that day admitted to any peccadilloes. A top broker with one of the country's largest houses, he told me, "What you said really hit home. Every day, I go to work thinking, 'My job is to lie. I lie to all my clients. Not big, black lies all the time, but lies that have to do with exaggeration and omission. If I didn't lie, I'd be unemployed.' That's how I rationalize what I do."

I told him that I admired his honesty and that he might be able to find a way out of his quandary by believing in a very simple proposition: that in the long run, he'd make plenty of money for himself and plenty of money for his business if he could forget about being the number one salesperson in his firm and begin to think about making sure that his customers benefited from him at least as much as he was benefiting from them.

"Think about what you'd like to get from a broker," I told him. "Then find a way to give your customers that . . . and then a little more."

Surely if he did that—and he could do that, for he was a smart, energetic, and resourceful person—he would gradually develop a Rolodex full of loyal, satisfied customers. The best thing about making sure your customers get as much or more out of your relationship as you do is that you don't have to keep finding new customers as the years go by. The old ones stay because they trust you, and they send their friends to you as well.

Following the "other guy first" policy not only guarantees success in the long run, it ensures that the dollars you earn later will come much more easily than the dollars you earn today.

In *Winners Never Cheat*, Huntsman tells a story about a deal he made with Emerson Kampen, CEO of Great Lakes Chemical Company in 1986. Huntsman agreed to sell 40 percent of a division of his company for $54 million. A handshake sealed the deal. Four months after the oral agreement, the documents were drafted. But during that time, the price of raw materials had decreased substantially and the profit margins of Huntsman's company were reaching all-time highs. Nothing had been signed and no documents had been exchanged. Kampen called him and proposed that instead of sticking with the $54 million they had orally agreed to, he would pay half of the $250 million the company had appreciated to. Huntsman told him no, that he was going to stick with his original deal.

"But that's not fair to you," Kampen responded.

"You negotiate for your company, Emerson, and let me negotiate for mine," Huntsman replied.

That's an amazing example of making sure your business associate gets at least as good a deal as you get. And that anecdote erased a good deal of the skepticism I had toward Huntsman when I opened his book.

As Larry King said in his foreword to *Winners Never Cheat*, "Leo Durocher was quite wrong when he said nice guys finish last. Not only can nice people finish first, they finish better."

In thinking about this principle recently, it's occurred to me that equity in business is the same as equity in personal relationships. It is the result of a long-term approach to value. If you want your marriage to last a long time, you must focus your energy on what you can do for your spouse, not what you can get from the marriage. The same is true in business. People who have trouble making long-term personal relationships are seldom able to develop long-term, appreciating businesses.

Thinking about the other guy first may not be instinctual behavior. But the course of human progress could be said to be the history of our efforts to do just that.

CHAPTER 11

Rich Man, Poor Man

﹏

*What can I say about my friend Richard Russell without using a lot
of superlatives? Richard has been writing and publishing the* Dow
Theory Letters *since 1958. This newsletter service holds the record
for being the longest continuously published newsletter by one
person in the investment business. Richard is now 81 years old and
still writes an extremely popular daily e-letter, full of commentary
on the markets and whatever interests him that day. He gets up at
3 a.m. or so and starts his massive daily reading, finishing the letter
just after the markets close. He is my business hero.*

*He was the first writer to recommend gold stocks in 1960. He
called the top of the 1949 to 1966 bull market, and called the
bottom of the bear market in 1974 almost to the day, predicting a
new bull market. (Think how tough it was to call for a bull market
in late 1974, when things looked really miserable!) He was a
bombardier in WWII, lived through the Depression, wars, and bull
and bear markets. I would say that Russell is another one of those
true innate market geniuses who have simply forgotten more than
most of us will ever know, except I am not certain he has forgotten
anything. His daily letter is loaded with references and wisdom
from the past and gives us a guide to the future. (You can learn
more at www.dowtheoryletters.com.)* —John Mauldin

﹏

Rich Man, Poor Man

by Richard Russell

MAKING MONEY ENTAILS A LOT MORE THAN PREDICTING WHICH WAY THE stock or bond markets are heading or trying to figure which stock or fund will double over the next few years. For the great majority of investors, making money requires a plan, self-discipline, and desire. I say "for the great majority of people," because if you're a Steven Spielberg or a Bill Gates you don't have to know about the Dow or the markets or about yields or price/earnings ratios. You're a phenomenon in your own field, and you're going to make big money as a byproduct of your talent and ability. But this kind of genius is rare.

The average investor—like you and me—needs to have a financial plan. Here, I'll offer some rules on investing that should be followed if you are serious about wanting to make money.

THE POWER OF COMPOUNDING

RULE #1
Compounding works.

One of the most important lessons for living in the modern world is that to survive you've got to have money. But to live (survive) happily, you must have love, health (mental and physical), freedom, intellectual stimulation—and money. When I taught my kids about money, the first thing I taught them was the use of the *money bible*. What's the money bible? Simple; it's a volume of the *compounding interest tables*.

Compounding is the royal road to riches. Compounding is the safe road, the sure road, and fortunately, anybody can do it. To compound successfully, you need the following: perseverance in order to keep you firmly on the savings path. You need intelligence in order to understand what you are doing and why. You need knowledge of the mathematical tables in order to comprehend the amazing rewards that will come to you if you faithfully follow the compounding road. And, of course, you need time, time to allow the power of compounding to work for you. Remember, compounding *only works through time*.

But there are two catches in the compounding process. The first is obvious—compounding may involve sacrifice (you can't spend it and still save it). Second, compounding is boring—b-o-r-i-n-g. Or I should say it's boring until (after seven or eight years) the money starts to pour in. Then, believe me, compounding becomes very interesting. In fact, it becomes downright fascinating!

In order to emphasize the power of compounding, I am including the following extraordinary study, courtesy of Market Logic, a newsletter by Norman Fosback.

In this study we assume that investor B opens an IRA at age 19. For seven consecutive periods he puts $2,000 into the IRA at an average growth rate of 10 percent (7 percent interest plus growth). After seven years, this fellow makes no more contributions—he's finished.

A second investor, A, makes no contributions until age 26 (this is the age when investor B was finished making contributions). Then A continues faithfully to contribute $2,000 every year until age 65 (at the same theoretical 10 percent rate).

Now study the incredible results show in Table 11.1. Investor B, who made contributions earlier and who made only seven contributions, ends up with more money than A, who made 40 contributions but at a *later time*. The difference in the two is that B had *seven more early years of compounding than A*. Those seven early years were worth more than all of A's 33 additional contributions.

	TABLE 11.1			

Power of Compounding: Investor A versus Investor B

	Investor A		Investor B	
Age	Contribution	Year-End Value	Contribution	Year-End Value
8	-0-	-0-	-0-	-0-
9	-0-	-0-	-0-	-0-
10	-0-	-0-	-0-	-0-
11	-0-	-0-	-0-	-0-
12	-0-	-0-	-0-	-0-
13	-0-	-0-	-0-	-0-
14	-0-	-0-	-0-	-0-
15	-0-	-0-	-0-	-0-
16	-0-	-0-	-0-	-0-
17	-0-	-0-	-0-	-0-
18	-0-	-0-	-0-	-0-
19	-0-	-0-	2,000	2,200
20	-0-	-0-	2,000	4,620
21	-0-	-0-	2,000	7,282
22	-0-	-0-	2,000	10,210
23	-0-	-0-	2,000	13,431
24	-0-	-0-	2,000	16,974
25	-0-	-0-	2,000	20,872
26	2,000	2,200	-0-	22,959
27	2,000	4,620	-0-	25,255
28	2,000	7,282	-0-	27,780
29	2,000	10,210	-0-	30,558
30	2,000	13,431	-0-	33,614
31	2,000	16,974	-0-	36,976
32	2,000	20,872	-0-	40,673
33	2,000	25,159	-0-	44,741
34	2,000	29,875	-0-	49,215
35	2,000	35,062	-0-	54,136
36	2,000	40,769	-0-	59,550
37	2,000	47,045	-0-	65,505
38	2,000	53,950	-0-	72,055
39	2,000	61,545	-0-	79,261
40	2,000	69,899	-0-	87,187
41	2,000	79,089	-0-	95,905
42	2,000	89,198	-0-	105,496
43	2,000	100,318	-0-	116,045
44	2,000	112,550	-0-	127,650
45	2,000	126,005	-0-	140,415

(Continued)

	Investor A			Investor B	
Age	Contribution	Year-End Value		Contribution	Year-End Value
46	2,000	140,805		-0-	154,456
47	2,000	157,086		-0-	169,902
48	2,000	174,995		-0-	186,892
49	2,000	194,694		-0-	205,581
50	2,000	216,364		-0-	226,140
51	2,000	240,200		-0-	248,754
52	2,000	266,420		-0-	273,629
53	2,000	295,262		-0-	300,992
54	2,000	326,988		-0-	331,091
55	2,000	361,887		-0-	364,200
56	2,000	400,276		-0-	400,620
57	2,000	442,503		-0-	440,682
58	2,000	488,953		-0-	484,750
59	2,000	540,049		-0-	533,225
60	2,000	596,254		-0-	586,548
61	2,000	658,079		-0-	645,203
62	2,000	726,087		-0-	709,723
63	2,000	800,896		-0-	780,695
64	2,000	883,185		-0-	858,765
65	2,000	973,704		-0-	944,641
Less Total Invested:		(80,000)			(14,000)
Equals Net Earnings:		893,704			930,641
Money Grew:		11-fold			66-fold

TABLE 11.1   *(Continued)*

Source: Market Logic

I suggest you show this study to your kids. It's a study I've lived by, and I can tell you, "It works." You can work your compounding with muni-bonds, with a good money market fund, with T-bills, or, say, with five-year T-notes.

RULE #2

Don't lose money.

This may sound naive, but believe me it isn't. If you want to be wealthy, you must not lose money, or I should say, you must not lose *big* money. Absurd rule, silly rule? Maybe, but *most people lose money* in disastrous investments, gambling, rotten business deals, greed, poor timing. Yes, after almost five decades of investing and talking to investors, I can tell you that most people definitely *do* lose money, lose big-time—in the stock market, in options and futures, in real estate, in bad loans, in mindless gambling, and in their own businesses.

RULE #3

Wealthy people don't need the markets.

In the investment world the wealthy investor has one major advantage over the little guy, the stock market amateur, and the neophyte trader. The advantage that wealthy investors enjoy is that they don't need the markets. I can't begin to tell you what a difference that makes, both in one's mental attitude and in the way one actually handles one's money.

Wealthy investors don't need the markets, because *they already have all the income they need.* Money is being generated from bonds, T-bills, money-market funds, stocks, and real estate. In other words, the wealthy investors *never feel pressured* to "make money" in the market.

Wealthy investors tend to be an expert on values. When bonds are cheap and bond yields are irresistibly high, they buy bonds. When stocks are on the bargain table and stock yields are attractive, they buy stocks. When real estate is a great value, they buy real estate. When great art or fine jewelry or gold is on the "giveaway" table, they buy art or diamonds or gold. In other words, the wealthy investor puts his money where the great values are.

And if no outstanding values are available, the wealthy investors *wait.* They have money coming in daily, weekly, monthly. They can afford to wait until a good investment comes along. This is known as patience.

But what about the little guy? This fellow always feels pressured to "make money." And in return, he's always pressuring the market to "do something" for him. But sadly, the market isn't interested. When the little guy isn't buying stocks offering 1 percent or 2 percent yields, he's off to Las Vegas or Atlantic City trying to beat the house at roulette. Or he's spending 20 bucks a week on lottery tickets, or he's "investing" in some crackpot scheme that his neighbor told him about (in strictest confidence, of course).

And because the little guy is trying to force the market to *do* something, he's a guaranteed loser. The little guy doesn't understand values, so he constantly overpays. He doesn't comprehend the power of compounding, and he doesn't understand money. He's never heard the adage, "He who understands interest, earns it. He who doesn't understand interest, pays it." The little guy is the typical American, and he's deeply in debt.

The little guy is in hock up to his ears. As a result, he's always sweating—sweating to make payments on his house, his refrigerator, his car, or his lawn mower. He's impatient, and he feels perpetually put upon. He tells himself that he has to make money—fast. And he dreams of those "big, juicy mega-bucks." In the end, the little guy wastes his money in the market, or he loses his money gambling, or he dribbles it away on senseless schemes. In short, this "money-nerd" spends life dashing up the financial down escalator.

But here's the ironic part of it. If, from the beginning, the little guy had adopted a strict policy of never spending more than he made, if he had taken his extra savings and compounded it in intelligent, income-producing securities, then in due time he'd have money coming in daily, weekly, monthly, just like the rich man. The little guy would have become a financial winner, instead of a pathetic loser.

RULE #4

Look for values.

The only time the average investor should stray outside the basic compounding system is when a given market offers outstanding value. I judge an investment to be a great value when it offers (a) safety; (b) an attractive return; and (c) a good chance of appreciating in price. At all other times, the compounding route is safer and probably a lot more profitable, at least in the long run.

THE TRICK IS TO BEAT TIME

Here's something you won't hear from your broker or read about in the "How to Beat the Market" books. All investing and speculation is basically an exercise in attempting to beat time.

When you try to pick the winning stock or when you try to sell out near the top of a bull market or when you try in-and-out trading, you may not realize it but what you're doing is trying to beat time.

Time is the single most valuable asset you can ever have in your investment arsenal. The problem is that none of us has enough of it.

But let's indulge in a bit of fantasy. Let's say you have 200 years to live, 200 years in which to invest. Here's what you could do. You could buy $20,000 worth of municipal bonds yielding, say, 5.5 percent.

At 5.5 percent percent, money doubles in thirteen years. So here's your plan: Each time your money doubles you add another $10,000. So at the end of thirteen years you have $40,000 plus the $10,000 you've added, meaning that at the end of thirteen years you have $50,000.

At the end of the next thirteen years you have $100,000, you add $10,000, and then you have $110,000. You reinvest it all in 5.5 percent munis, and at the end of the next thirteen years you have $220,000 and you add $10,000, making it $230,000.

At the end of the next thirteen years you have $460,000 and you add $10,000, making it $470,000.

In 200 years there are 15.3 doubles. You do the math. By the end of the 200th year you wouldn't know what to do with all your money. It would be coming out of your ears. And all with minimum risk.

So with enough time, you would be rich—guaranteed. You wouldn't have to waste any time picking the right stock or the right group or the right mutual fund. You would just compound your way to riches, using your greatest asset: time.

There's only one problem: in the real world you're not going to live 200 years. But if you start young enough or if you start your kids early, you or they might have anywhere from thirty to sixty years of time ahead of you.

Because most people have run out of time, they spend endless hours and nervous energy trying to beat time, which, by the way, is really what investing is all about. Pick a stock that advances from 3 to 100, and if you've put enough money in that stock you'll have beaten time. Or join a company that gives you a million options, and your option moves up from 3 to 25, and again you've beaten time.

How about this real example of beating time: John Walter joined AT&T, but after nine short months he was out of a job. The complaint was that Walter "lacked intellectual leadership." Walter got $26 million for that little stint in a severance package. That's what you call really beating time. Of course, a few of us might have another word for it—and for AT&T.

IN THE MARKETS, HOPE IS
THE DANGEROUS SIREN SONG

It's human nature to be optimistic. It's human nature to hope. Furthermore, hope is a component of a healthy state of mind. Hope is the opposite of negativity. Negativity in life can lead to anger, disappointment, and depression. After all, if the world is a negative place, what's the point of living in it? To be negative is to be anti-life.

Ironically, it doesn't work that way in the stock market. In the stock market, hope is a hindrance, not a help. Once you take a position in a stock, you obviously want that stock to advance. But if the stock you bought is a real value, and you bought it right, you should be content to sit with that stock in the knowledge that over time its value will rise without your help, without your hoping.

So in the case of this stock, you have value on your side—and all you need is patience. In the end, your patience will pay off with a higher price for your stock. Hope shouldn't play any part in this process. You don't need hope, because you bought the stock when it was a great value, and you bought it at the right time.

Any time you find yourself hoping in this business, the odds are that you are on the wrong path—or that you did something stupid that should be corrected.

Unfortunately, hope is a money-loser in the investment business. This is counterintuitive but true. Hope will keep you riding a stock that is headed down. Hope will keep you from taking a small loss and, instead, allowing that small loss to develop into a large loss.

In the stock market hope gets in the way of reality, hope gets in the way of common sense. One of the first rules in investing is "Don't take the big loss." In order to do that, you've got to be willing to take a small loss.

If the stock market turns bearish, and you're staying put with your whole position, and you're *hoping* that what you see is not really happening—then welcome to poverty city. In this situation, all your hoping isn't going to save you or make you a penny. In fact, in this situation hope is the devil that bids you to sit—while your portfolio of stocks goes down the drain.

In the investing business my suggestion is that you avoid hope. Forget the siren, hope; instead, embrace cold, clear reality.

THERE IS NO SUBSTITUTE FOR ACTION

A few days ago a young subscriber asked me, "Russell, you've been dealing with the markets since the late 1940s. This is a strange question, but what is the most important lesson you've learned in all that time?"

I didn't have to think too long. I told him, "The most important lesson I've learned comes from something Freud said. He said, 'Thinking is rehearsing.' What Freud meant was that thinking is no substitute for acting. In this world, in investing, in any field, there is no substitute for taking action."

This brings up another story that illustrates the same theme. J. P. Morgan was "Master of the Universe" back in the 1920s. One day a young man came up to Morgan and said, "Mr. Morgan, I'm sorry to bother you, but I own some stocks that have been acting poorly, and I'm very anxious about these stocks. In fact, worrying about those stocks is starting to ruin my health. Yet, I still like the stocks. It's a terrible dilemma. What do you think I should do, sir?"

Without hesitating Morgan said, "Young man, sell to the sleeping point."

The lesson is the same. There's no substitute for acting. In the business of investing or the business of life, thinking is not going to do it for you. Thinking is just rehearsing. You must learn to act.

That's the single most important lesson that I've learned in this business.

Again, and I've written about this episode before, a very wealthy and successful investor once said to me, "Russell, do you know why stockbrokers never become rich in this business?"

I confessed that I didn't know. He explained, "They don't get rich because they never believe their own bull."

Again, it's the same lesson. If you want to make money (or get rich) in a bull market, thinking and talking isn't going to do it. You've got to buy stocks. Brokers never do that. Do you know one broker who has?

A painful lesson: Back in 1991 when we had a perfect opportunity, we could have ended Saddam Hussein's career, and we could have done it with ease. But those in command, for political reasons, didn't want to face the adverse publicity of taking additional U.S. casualties. So we stopped short, and Saddam was home free. We were afraid to act. And now we're dealing with that failure to act with another and messier war.

In my own life, many of the mistakes I've made have come because I forgot or ignored the "acting lesson." Thinking is rehearsing, and I was rehearsing instead of acting. Bad marriages, bad investments, lost opportunities, bad business decisions—they are all made worse because we fail for any number of reasons to act.

The reasons to act are almost always better than the reasons you can think up not to act. If you, my dear readers, can understand the meaning of what is expressed in this one sentence, then believe me, you've learned a most valuable lesson. It's a lesson that has saved my life many times. And I mean literally, it's a lesson that has saved my life.

CHAPTER 12

The Millennium Wave

As a recognized expert and leader on investment issues, Millennium Wave Investments President John Mauldin is primarily involved in private money management, financial services, and investments. John Mauldin is a prolific author, writer, and editor of the popular Thoughts from the Frontline *e-letter, which goes to more than 1,500,000 readers weekly and is posted on numerous independent Web sites. He is the author of the best-selling* Bull's Eye Investing. *He also writes a free letter on hedge funds and private offerings for accredited investors.*

John demonstrates an unusual breadth of expertise, as illustrated by the wide variety of issues addressed in-depth in his writings. He has a unique ability to present complex financial topics and make them understandable to the lay reader. His background includes a wide variety of studies and experiences, and he has traveled extensively, visiting well over forty countries and forty-eight states. A popular public speaker, John addresses numerous investment conferences and seminars.

John Mauldin is an Arlington, Texas, businessman, and the father of seven children, ranging from ages 11 through 28, five of whom are adopted. His offices are in right field of the Ballpark in Arlington. (To learn more about him, go to www.johnmauldin.com.)

In this chapter, John explains why we are entering a decade where change will come faster and be more profound than at any time in history. In fact, there are numerous waves of change that are all joining together to form what he calls the Millennium Wave, a period of accelerating change at the beginning of this millennium—which will be the single largest period of transformation in human history.

The Millennium Wave

by John Mauldin

"It will therefore be crucial that you see the world anew. That means looking from the outside in to reanalyze much that you have probably taken for granted. This will enable you to come to an understanding. If you fail to transcend conventional thinking at a time when conventional thinking is losing touch with reality, then you will be more likely to fall prey to an epidemic of disorientation that lies ahead. Disorientation breeds mistakes that could threaten your business, your investments and your way of life."
—James Dale Davidson and
Lord William Rees-Mogg,
The Sovereign Individual, in 1997

OVER THE NEXT TEN TO TWELVE YEARS, WE WILL SEE THREE RECESSIONS THAT will slowly move the average price-to-earnings ratio of stocks to historic lows. Rising oil and energy prices will be a main culprit of both the slowdown in the economy and an increase in inflation. Ever-increasing monetary inflation will, in fact, trigger a huge increase in all commodity prices, as well as a decline in bonds. Asset inflation will show up in the housing markets as home values continue to skyrocket. The dollar will continue to weaken against major foreign currencies. The current war will become increasingly unpopular, and the next administration will be forced to withdraw troops, under guise of declaring victory. The American voting public will be split as never before, with major patterns in voting habits making a generational change. The newspapers will continue to write about how an Asian country will dominate the world economically in less than a few decades.

Following this period of malaise, there will be an amazing cycle of new technical innovation that will spark yet another major bull market. The new technologies will change the world in ways that simply cannot now be imagined and will lead to whole new industries, putting amazing new power and abilities into the hands of individuals and governments.

The preceding scenario would, in fact, all come to pass. Except that the year was 1970 and not today. The forces that have changed the world in the decades following 1970 were only written about in science fiction and a few obscure books and journals. Who dreamed of the Internet in 1970? Who could envision that the Berlin Wall would come down in 1989? That Japan would not, in fact, dominate the world of economics and overwhelm the United States? Or that the China of Mao would become a capitalistic growth machine and that the USSR would break up? A personal computer on every desk and more computing power in an automobile than existed in the largest computers of the time? A globalized world economy? The prospect that a falling population (and not overcrowding) would be a problem, or that a Green Revolution would mean enough food for all (except where governments kept out a free market)?

In the 1970s, the mood of the country was decidedly negative. Japan was eroding our manufacturing base and unemployment was increasing. Reagan spoke of the Misery Index in his race against Jimmy Carter, which was a combination of inflation and unemployment.

And yet it all changed. In fact, the one constant in the modern world is that the pace of change is accelerating.

"My interest is in the future, because I am going to spend the rest of my life here."

—Charles F. Kettering

In his groundbreaking book, *The Third Wave*, Alvin Toffler depicted the First Wave as the agricultural revolution, the Second

Wave as the industrial revolution, and the Third Wave as the electronic data and communication revolution. He depicted a society that would be working in "electronic hamlets" sending their daily work over "electronic highways" to "virtual places of business."

Written twenty-five years ago, *The Third Wave* was an amazingly prescient book. Toffler saw a world of mass customization, with government and business interwoven and a world filled with ambiguity and change. Although some suggest that we're still in the middle of Toffler's Third Wave, I would suggest that what we are facing is different in both substance and character.

The Third Wave was actually the result of an innovation cycle that we can call the *Information Age.* I believe we are only halfway through the Information Age, with more profound changes as to how we work and play just around the corner.

But this time something is different. Instead of one wave of innovation following another, I believe that we are going to see multiple waves of significant change and innovation surge all over the world at roughly the same time. The combined effects are going to produce a period of change unlike anything seen in the history of man.

I call the combination of these factors *the Millennium Wave.* It will change things in ways that almost defy the imagination and at a pace that will leave one breathless. On the one hand, the Millennium Wave will be seen as a source of good, as we will live healthier and longer and there will be more of the basic necessities of life and more life options. On the other hand, the very ground we walk on will seem like it is shifting. The roadmap we have in our mind for our future will require a constant fine-tuning (if not major reprogramming) in order to determine our position.

The more precisely you plan your future, the harder that change will hit you. Flexibility will be the order of the day. To paraphrase the prayer from Alcoholics Anonymous, "Please grant me the knowledge of what will change, the understanding of what will not change, and the wisdom to understand the difference."

As I pondered the question I put to the other writers in this book, "What is the one thing you have learned that you want to pass on?" I came to realize that the key talent in the future would be the ability to deal with the tremendous technological and cultural changes that are coming at an ever-increasing pace while developing an understanding of how those changes will evolve in the age-old patterns of life. There are patterns that change very slowly or cycle or trend. Learning how all these patterns fit together with the changes of the Millennium Wave is at the heart of not just the investment enterprise, but modern life in general.

But let's deal with the investment enterprise first. Anyone familiar with the research on the psychology of investing knows that it points to the overwhelming conclusion that the broad class of investors (which does not include you or me, of course) consistently assumes that the current trend will continue long into the future.

They may give lip service to believing things will change, they may constantly worry about changing trends, but they do not invest that way. The late and deservedly famous economist Herbert Stein taught us the simple concept: "An unsustainable trend will not be sustained." And yet investors (and indeed all humans on almost every level) allow the current trend to be the primary force in their vision of the future. As Mark Finn noted in Chapter 3, we use past performance, even when we know we shouldn't, to be the guide for picking our future investments.

Investors all too often rationalize their actions with the mantra of "this time it's different" or assume they will be able to nimbly react to or avoid the effects of the change when it happens. It never is and they hardly ever do.

My personal career path has been one of almost constant change. Yet it is but an echo of a million other entrepreneurs and businessmen and women. We all deal with change. In fact, the amount of change that I have had to deal with is rather unremarkable, in the grand scheme of things. There are millions—perhaps billions—of people who go through far more abrupt changes almost daily.

How well we deal with life (not just our investments!) in the next thirty-five years is going to be directly related to how well we deal with what will be an accelerating pace in the rate of change.

My personal experience of continuing change will be echoed throughout the world. Some of the changes were forced upon me.

Some of them I willingly embraced. I have told my friends on several of these changes that I hope this is the last time I have to "reinvent" myself. I succumb to the fantasy that most investors have: that the trend of today will continue. And yet, I know that this is not likely. The field in which I plow and reap is changing rapidly, and it is unlikely that in ten years it will even look the same.

When I began my career thirty years ago, there was no fax, no overnight delivery, and phone service was expensive. Computers? Not until twenty years ago, and they were toys compared to today's machines. It cost a lot of money to deliver a newsletter up until just a few years ago. Now the marginal cost is almost nothing. One or one million is pretty much the same to me.

Research was a visit to the library, in addition to a personal collection of books and a few magazines and newsletters. Now I get scores of letters and articles every day delivered to my "mailbox," plus an almost infinite amount of data at my fingertips using something called Google. I have almost five gigabytes of research and articles stored from just the past few years on my computer, which I can search with a few strokes. To write an eight- to ten-page weekly letter as I do would have taken a week with a month to research just a decade ago. Now I can access huge amounts of data each week, and I write my weekly letter on a computer in about five hours on a Friday afternoon. (I read where they will soon have pills that will help our memories. I am going to need them.)

International readers? Very few ever graced my musings in the last decade. Now, I have thousands of international readers, often from some amazingly remote locations.

In short, the changes have been dramatic. At times, I complain, it has been hard to adjust. A lot of times those changes were just plain not fun. Some of them were very expensive lessons. Yet, I continue on down my current business path. But I know that change is coming. *Change is like a train. It can either run over you, or you can catch it to the future.*

But I can hear that peasant from China, as he follows an ox on the way to the city, telling me I can't even begin to imagine the speed of change. Think about the changes in China and Russia or other parts of the developing world in the last ten years.

My less-than-sainted Dad last hitched a wagon to drive to town in the 1920s. He saw a man put on the moon with a slide rule, a yellow pad, and pencils forty years later. That pace of change has only increased.

In 1967, the movie *The Graduate* was the hit of the season. We remember that famous scene where a young Benjamin Braddock (Dustin Hoffman) was told to seek a career in plastics. That was the rage at the time. But it turns out that was bad advice. Over 40 percent of jobs in plastics have disappeared since 1967.

And yet, there has been plenty of job growth. There were clearly better opportunities than plastics. Princeton Professor Alan Krueger tells us a quarter of all workers are now in occupations that were not listed in the Census Bureau's occupation codes in 1967.[1] In 1967, if asked where the jobs and opportunities were going to come from, the proper and correct answer would have been, "I don't know, but they will." It is still the correct answer today.

Personal computers were yet a dream. AT&T was still a monopoly. Fiber optics? The Internet? Cell phones? Robotics? Biotech? Global positioning? Faxes? Video? MP3? Computer-aided design? They didn't exist.

In less than thirty years, we will look back at the changes that are still in our future and realize they were far, even vastly, more revolutionary than what we have seen in the last thirty. But just as in 1975, when it would be hard to imagine the coming changes, in 2005 it is even harder to imagine what 2035 will be. We delude ourselves into thinking we know, but we really don't. The truly amazing things and inventions are still not even on a drawing board or in a garage.

There is plenty of entrepreneurial activity in the world, and the future foundation for large companies that will reward their investors is even now being laid. The driver for the next Microsoft, eBay, or Amgen will be the new opportunities brought about by the pace of change.

What kind of pace of change are we talking about? Ray Kurzweil, the inventor of speech recognition, scanners, music synthesizers and many other technical marvels, has a team of ten who track the progress of technology and predict where it will be in ten or twenty or one hundred years. He is an unabashed enthusiast when it comes to thinking about the future. It helps that he has been right so far, so it behooves us to pay attention when he notes (this was written in 2001):

> The first technological steps—sharp edges, fire, the wheel—took tens of thousands of years. For people living in this era, there was little noticeable technological change in even a thousand years. By 1000 A.D., progress was much faster and a paradigm shift required only a century or two. In the nineteenth century, we saw more technological change than in the nine centuries preceding it. Then in the first twenty years of the twentieth century, we saw more advancement than in all of the nineteenth century. Now, paradigm shifts occur in only a few years time. The World Wide Web did not exist in anything like its current form just a few years ago; it didn't exist at all a decade ago.
>
> "The paradigm shift rate (i.e., the overall rate of technical progress) is currently doubling (approximately) every decade; that is, paradigm shift times are halving every decade (and the rate of acceleration is itself growing exponentially). So, the technological progress in the twenty-first century will be equivalent to what would require (in the linear view) on the order of two hundred centuries. In contrast, the twentieth century saw only about twenty-five years of progress (again at today's rate of progress) since we have been speeding up to current rates. So the twenty-first century will see almost a thousand times greater technological change than its predecessor."[2]

What Ray is saying is that most people project future growth in technology at today's rate of change. But the rate of change is accelerating, so that more and more change is packed into smaller and smaller amounts of time. Although the vast majority of the thousand times greater technological change Ray is talking about happens in the last part of this century, some of it happens in the next twenty years. How much change are we talking about? Well, from when he first penned those words, the pace of change has picked up. At current levels, that means the twentieth century was equivalent to about twenty years of progress at to-day's rate of change. That pace will continue to increase the amount of innovation we pack into just a few years. From his book *Fantastic Voyage*:

> . . . And we'll make another twenty years of progress at today's rate [of growth], equivalent to that of the entire twentieth century, in the next fourteen years. And then we'll do it again in just seven years.

That means in the next twenty-one years we will see double the technological change that we saw in the entire twentieth century. At that pace, we will see almost four times the rate of change within twenty-five years.

How can this be? To get an idea, during the week I finalized this essay, the *Wall Street Journal* ran a front-page story about the most recent project of J. Craig Venter. Venter was the president of Celera, the private project to generate a copy of the human genome. Using much newer and faster equipment than the government-sponsored project, Celera achieved its goal in just two years.

The parts of a DNA synthesizer can now be purchased for $10,000. Rob Carlson speculates that by 2010 a single person will be able to sequence or synthesize tens of millions of sequence bases a day. Within a decade, a single person could sequence or synthesize all the DNA describing all the people on the planet many times over in an eight-hour day—or sequence his own DNA in seconds.

So what is Venter doing now? He has taken his fortune made in Celera and is going to create an artificial life form. We have been able to splice genes into a cell or bacteria for three decades. Venter intends to start from scratch, creating his own entirely new life form. He expects to succeed in a few years.[3]

When he (or those who are in competition with him) succeeds, we will have a building block to start adding new functionalities. Venter imagines a bacteria that would chew up cellulose and turn it into ethanol. Another could turn sunlight into hydrogen. The list is endless.

Today, 99 percent of drugs in existence are created in what is basically a trial and error format. We test substance after substance, trying to find a use for it. Will this one stop a cancer or decrease blood pressure? Every now and then we find one, but we often don't really know why it works on a molecular level. It is crude and expensive. What Venter and a thousand others like him are trying to do is figure out the programming for the DNA and RNA sequences.

Wouldn't it be nice to turn off the gene that causes us to store fat? This gene was quite useful ten thousand years ago, but today it is a health hazard. Or stop the genetic process that causes the arteries to harden? Or as Venter speculates, turn our grass clippings into clean-burning fuel for our cars?

As our knowledge expands, as our tools grow in number and decrease in cost, our ability to find useful products increases at an ever-growing rate. The tool that Venter will create will allow for all sorts of new products and discoveries.

And that is just one small tool. There are thousands of such tools, big and small, being created by scientists and inventors in research labs all over the world every month in scores of different industries. Each one allows the next group of inventors to create even more and better tools and ultimately products. As we will note below, globalization is not just a manufacturing and sales process. It is also an intellectual process, as scientists from many parts of the globe can collaborate on a project, each bringing a specialized part of knowledge to the project. That allows scientists in smaller countries or in countries without significant resources to add to the sum total or brainpower being thrown at a project.

All this will mean change is going to come faster than ever before. But faster technological change does not mean that everything changes.

La plus ca change, la plus c'est la meme chose.
The more things change, the more things stay the same.

What of the future? Can we really stand here in 2005 and have some idea of what will transpire in the next two to three decades? Looking at which things will not change will give us some clues as to what will change, and some ideas as to the future in which we and our children will assuredly live.

There are three things that over the next forty years are not going to change.

The innovation cycle is not going to change—it will be with us as it is simply part of our human progression, although it is going to increase in intensity and frequency.

The business cycle and its cousins, secular bull and bear markets, will not change. As long as the business cycle remains in place (and Congress has yet to find a way to repeal it), this tendency to go from overvalued to undervalued markets that started when the Medes were trading with the Persians, will persist.

Human psychology is not going to change. Human psychology is the reason we get these cycles, and the reason we get busts and booms.

THE INNOVATION CYCLE

A Russian economist, Nikolas Kondratieff, noticed that we can look at cycles in the markets, and his research led to these long waves becoming known as the Kondratieff Wave.[4] Many argued that these up-and-down cycles lasted 56 years, 73 years, or 69.3 years. Most people, including me, look at that research and think that it is voodoo economics. What is implied by many of the adherents of the K-Wave theory is that the markets and actual prices themselves are predetermined in some fixed, almost linear, fashion, like a predetermined destiny in a science fiction novel. The Kondratieff Wave followers were the guys that were telling you, if you were reading the sales letters published in the late 1980s, about the crash of 1990, the crash of 1987 or the crash of 1994.

The Kondratieff Wave disciples tried to predict market direction with a precise cycle determining the precise numbers of years, and when they dated the beginning of the last cycle. They had figured out that there were in fact cycles, but Joseph Schumpeter came along and said the cycles really relate more to innovation cycles than fixed waves in time.

What Schumpeter found was that a new innovation takes a great deal of time to get to a 10 percent penetration in any given market, but the growth from 10 percent to 90 percent is one of rapid change. The cycle follows what we call an S-Curve, and as you get to the mature phase (or the last 10 percent of growth), everyone eventually gets access to the innovation. The innovation now has complete penetration and growth slows until it is basically in line with the economy's growth, which is GDP (gross domestic product) plus inflation. The innovation can go into other places where it hasn't penetrated, but once it has saturated the major world economies like the United States or Europe, it is no longer an innovation, but a commodity. Its price goes down as more and more firms can produce the product.

Harry Dent came along and said let's rework this innovation cycle idea a little bit and try to define it better. Although his book *The Roaring 2000s*[5] is an excellent analysis of the innovation cycle, please pay no attention to the investment projections that he makes, like the Dow going to 40,000 by 2008. What he says is that when you look back over time, there are five phases to the innovation cycle. First is the innovation period, second a growth boom followed by a shakeout, then the maturity phase, and then the ending or final phase.

What happens during the shakeout is that a frenzy develops where too many people are throwing money at the innovation, overbuilding, and adding way too much capacity, because that's what we as humans do. We chase what is already hot rather than what might become hot in the future. We throw money at stuff that's going up, create too much of it, and then there's not enough market demand for that capacity and you get a shakeout. It happens almost invariably in all innovation cycles.

The words "this time it is different" are spoken. We project current trends far into the future, not realizing that overbuilding will cause prices to collapse.

We are all familiar with the overdevelopment of transocean fiber optic capacity. The first few lines were projected to have (and some actually did have) fabulous profit potential. But then everyone jumped in and too much capacity was built, forcing a dramatic drop in price.

This is not far different from railroads. When the first twenty-mile railroad was built in England, the investors found their profit projections were way off. Profits were much higher than anticipated. In fact, the early railroads were showing 100 percent profit in the first year. Just like fiber optics 150 years later, too many railroads were built and bankruptcies were soon the order of the day. There were hundreds of automobile manufacturing companies in the first part of the twentieth century and thousands of phone companies. As I said, it happens with almost every new major innovation.

But over time, demand catches up with supply, and (using our railroad example) more railroads were needed and the maturity boom took over. While hard for the initial investors, it was actually good for society, as all that capacity and lower prices meant new business opportunities developed as whole new markets opened up. The same thing will happen with transoceanic fiber optics. One day, as incredulous as it seems now, there will be another building wave of transoceanic fiber (or its futuristic equivalent).

As an example, right now, in my opinion, we are still in the growth boom of the information age. We haven't seen the true shakeout yet. No one knows how the development of broadband to U.S. homes will play out. Will it be on cable or fiber or even on your power lines? Who will be your phone/cable/wireless/cell/Internet/entertainment company in ten years? What bundled services will we all feel we need? The dot-com era was a precursor to the potential shakeout coming. When we see the true information age shakeout, I think it will look like all classic growth boom shakeouts. We will see too much capacity, and prices will plummet. Some major companies will not survive; others will stand tall. The excess capacity will soon be swallowed up in growing demand and then this Information Age innovation cycle will start its mature boom phase.

When you are looking at change, remember that the Innovation Cycle will be how that change comes about. You don't have to be there at the beginning, but when the new innovation shows its head, you need to invest with a view to the longer term. And remember that when there is too much of a good thing, it is time to sit on the sidelines. My bet is that the innovation cycles of the Millennium Wave will be much shorter in duration (products going to full market penetration) than those of the past.

SECULAR BULL AND SECULAR BEAR MARKETS

Another cycle that will always be there is the business cycle, accompanied by secular bull and secular bear investment markets. We use secular, not in the terms of religion, but from the Latin word *secula*, which means an age or period of time. What I argue in my book *Bull's Eye Investing* is that we shouldn't look at these cycles in terms of price, which most people do, but rather we should look at them in terms of valuation.

Michael Alexander wrote a great, though often overlooked, book called *Stock Cycles* in 1999. In it, he says, "Here's why we're going to have this crash," completely apart from everything else. He seems to have pegged the markets with the way he views cycles. Alexander finds that valuation cycles in secular bear/bull markets run anywhere from eight to seventeen years, which suggests that we're currently in the middle innings of a secular bear cycle. In the past, a secular bear never stopped in the middle of going down; it always went to the full extent of the pendulum. There will be bull market rallies during a secular bear market, but the next secular bull market will begin after we go through what I call *The Puke Factor*, when very few want to talk about or own equities anymore.

The race is not always to the swift or the battle to the strong, but that is the way to bet. You don't want to make a long-shot bet on the slowest horse winning when you are going to a horse race. You want to look for the horse that is likely to win that day. History shows us that bear markets always start with high price-to-earnings (P/E) ratios and bull markets always start with low P/E ratios. The lower the P/E ratio at the beginning of the period, the higher your returns are going to be when the P/E ratio tops out.

Where (in terms of P/E) you start investing makes a huge difference as to what your results are going to be over time. In fact, there have been periods of twenty years or more that a market index has made zero real (after inflation) returns. That's not what the guys tell you down at the office when they are trying to get your money into their mutual fund. There's never a money manager that will tell you that today is not a good day to invest in their fund. It's always a good day to invest, although history shows us that some days are better than others.

Let's look at a study done by Jeremy Grantham, where he breaks up the years from 1925 to 2001 by looking at the average price-to-earnings level for the year (see Figure 12.1). He then groups the years based on this valuation into five different buckets. The highest P/E years was labeled the "most expensive 20 percent of history"; the lowest P/E years was labeled the "cheapest 20 percent of history." What he found is that over the next ten years the cheapest or second cheapest quintiles had an average compound return of 11 percent. That's when your financial planner tells you to write a 10 percent to 12 percent return expectation into your retirement planning model, saying, "Look, see what the market has done for the past ten to fifteen years?"

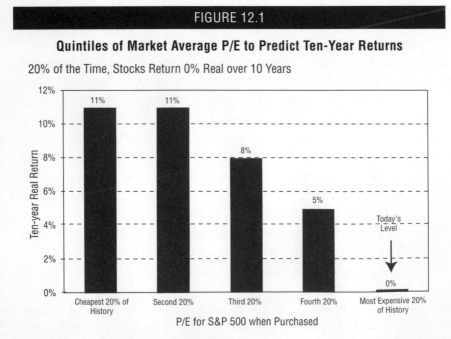

FIGURE 12.1

Quintiles of Market Average P/E to Predict Ten-Year Returns

20% of the Time, Stocks Return 0% Real over 10 Years

Source: GMO, Standard & Poor's. Data: 1925–2001

However, if you invested in the most expensive quintile in history, the average compound return over the next ten years was zero. That's not a good deal, except for the managers charging a fee to manage your money. So, getting into the market during times of low valuations has been the best choice in the past.

Again, this cycle between high and low valuations in unlikely to change. It is driven by human psychology. Using this cycle to inform your investment behavior will result in much more favorable returns.

Markets are volatile. What you find is that over the last 103 years the Dow Jones Industrial Average's annual return was between +/− 10 percent around 30 percent of the time. Over 70 percent of the time, the annual return was either above 10 percent or below 10 percent.[6] A company called Dalbar has done some studies that show the average investor does not do nearly as well as the average mutual fund does because they chase returns.[7] They switch into a fund that is "hot." Chasing returns is momentum investing—if something goes up, let's invest in it. What happens is, people typically get into something at the top, then it turns down and they get out. This strategy is essentially a formula for buy high, sell low, and is a poor way to invest. It is a result of investors projecting past performance into the future.

Let's talk about the real effect of compounding. Take the last 103 years from 1900 to 2002. The market's simple annual arithmetic average return is 7.2 percent. That's what the brokers and other salespeople are trotting out when they try and raise money. The problem is, over the same period of time, if the returns are compounded annually, the average is only 4.8 percent. Keep in mind that this is the compound average over long periods of time (in this case, 103 years). This negative compounding effect, if you will, stems from the fact that if you are down 33 percent early on, you are going to have to make 50 percent to bring you back (see Table 12.1).

At my Web site, www.2000wave.com, there are four charts for investment returns over the last 103 years (showing you the effects of taxes, inflation, and commissions). You can see in this chart what your returns would have been for any given period of time starting with any year you choose. The chart is color-coded;

TABLE 12.1

Average of the Years vs. Compounded Average
(Compounded Returns Are Adversely Affected by Negative Years and Volatility)

Simple Annual Returns

	'00	'01	'02	'03	'04	'05	'06	'07	'08	'09	Average
1900	7%	-9%	0%	-24%	42%	38%	-2%	-38%	47%	15%	
1910	-18%	0%	8%	-10%	-31%	82%	-4%	-22%	11%	30%	
1920	-33%	13%	22%	-3%	26%	30%	0%	29%	48%	-17%	
1930	-34%	-53%	-23%	67%	4%	39%	25%	-33%	28%	-3%	
1940	-13%	-15%	8%	14%	12%	27%	-8%	2%	-2%	13%	
1950	18%	14%	8%	-4%	44%	21%	2%	-13%	34%	16%	Average = 7.2%
1960	-9%	19%	-11%	17%	15%	11%	-19%	15%	4%	-15%	
1970	5%	6%	15%	-17%	-28%	38%	18%	-17%	-3%	4%	
1980	15%	-9$	20%	20%	-4%	28%	23%	2%	12%	27%	
1990	-4%	20%	4%	14%	2%	33%	26%	23%	16%	25%	
2000	-6%	-7%	-17%								

Compounded Annual Returns

	01/01/1990	12/31/2002	Average
Start	66.08		
End		8,341.63	→ Average = 4.8%
Years		103	

the reds are below-zero returns; pink is between zero and 3 percent; blue is between 3 percent and 7 percent, and light and dark green cover the periods with annual compounded returns over 7 percent. The annually compounded numbers are in white or black and indicate whether the price to earnings ratios were falling or rising during that period.

Surprise, surprise—you find out that almost all the light and dark green squares are periods of rising price to earnings ratios, or black numbers. However, the red and pink squares are predominately periods of contracting price to earnings ratios, or white numbers. This graph also helps visualize the long-term historical returns patterns in the market. You can easily find periods of ten or fifteen years where you're making 0 to 3 percent net. This tells me that when I see a period of high P/E valuations, better returns might be found elsewhere.

There is always a bull market somewhere in something. When you're in secular bear cycles, become more concerned about protecting against a loss and try for absolute returns; when you're in secular bull cycles, buying an index for relative returns has historically done well in the past. What I mean by that is, if price to earnings are at low valuations and you put money in index funds historically you will do well even if there are events like October 1987, because as the P/E rises it will, we hope, be due to the price going up rather than earnings coming down. All you need to do is follow the market because the market's going up, and if you actually beat the market by active management, you did a good job.

Now, if we are in a secular bear cycle, you want to do just the opposite. In secular bears, market valuations are going down over time. Now you want to focus on absolute returns and the need to protect against negative returns. Your measure, in a secular bear cycle, is a money market fund. In a secular bear cycle, the person who loses the least is the winner. That's just the way things are. Typically, you could have beaten stock market index returns dramatically in this period simply by being in bonds.

If you are under the age of 30, the good news for you is that you will probably get to see at least two more bull markets. Since average cycles are about thirteen years, you will see the end of the current bear, followed by what I think will be a rather large bull market. You are also young enough to see one more complete cycle prior to being 75 (which will seem young in another forty-five years, trust me!). Save every penny now and let them compound over time!

HUMAN PSYCHOLOGY

Human psychology, for better or worse, will always be with us. Developed over millennia, it is unlikely to change in the course of just a few years. The 2002 winners of the Nobel Prize for Economics were two psychologists (Daniel Kahneman and Vernon L. Smith), who came up with the sometimes-obvious idea that investors are irrational. Their contribution, however, was that humans are not just irrational, but predictably irrational. We keep on making the same mistakes time and again. I am reminded of one of my favorite quotes from Alfred Einstein, "Insanity is doing the same thing over and over and expecting different results."

It is this predictable irrationality that causes us to become irrationally exuberant and thus prone to creating investment bubbles, or groundlessly fearful, avoiding good value. Human psychology is at the root of secular bull and bear markets. It is also at the root of the innovation cycle, causing us to overbuild in moments of enthusiasm, always to the cry of "this time it's different."

I encourage you to read Chapter 6 on the Psychology of Investing by James Montier in this book, to learn why we make the mistakes we do. And then stop doing them! But also realize that your fellow human beings will look at the trends and cycles I discuss in the next section and, quite predictably, make the same mistakes over and over. There will be more bubbles in your future. Enjoy them. They can be great wealth builders if you don't get caught up in the hype. Remember, it is almost never different this time. And that goes double for trends that are driven by human emotions. We never learn.

SURFING THE MILLENNIUM WAVE

The Millennium Wave is a combination of multiple innovation waves coupled with profound societal changes, all happening at an accelerating pace of change that is unprecedented in human history. Although we cannot deal with each smaller wave in detail in this small chapter, let's briefly look at the components of the Millennium Wave. I think these will be positive forces that will help us get through the problems brought on by other aspects of the Millennium Wave.

As I already noted, I think in another few years that we will see a shakeout of the Information Age and then a follow-on maturity boom that will last another twenty years. Looking at past such cycles, the boom should be every bit as big as the innovation boom was in 1980 to 2005. That, in and of itself, will create an even greater worldwide technology and productivity boom, creating jobs and wealth.

Such a boom is not all that hard to forecast, and it will be welcome. But I think there is a surprise coming, something that we have not seen in human history. I believe we will get multiple major innovation booms overlaid on top of the maturity boom of the Information Age.

Currently, the Biotech Revolution is still in its initial innovation phase. It has barely made an impact in comparison to what most experts think it will in the next fifteen to twenty years. In another few years, we will start to see the beginning of the growth boom from the Biotech Revolution kick in. Amazing new drugs and processes will change the way we live. We will live longer and healthier lives, eat better and less expensive foods, clean up our waste (and our waists), and even develop new energy sources.

The Biotech Revolution promises to be far more life-changing than the Information Age, generating a wide array of new companies with technologies for extending our lives, preventing and healing diseases, and more efficiently feeding and clothing us. There are many of us who are at mid-life today who will live to see a robust 100 years. My children will be part of the first generation to celebrate the coming of two centuries, thanks to the life-enhancing and life-prolonging drugs and biotechnologies that lay just around the corner. And it will happen faster than most people currently think. Remember, the pace of innovation and change is accelerating.

Coming right on the heels of the Biotech Revolution will be the Quantum Revolution and nanotechnology—a world of unbelievably small machines and processes. What sounds like science fiction to-day will be reality in twenty to thirty years. Let me give just one small example. I read science fiction for relaxation, and have done so for forty-five years. There is a significant change in the subject matter of science fiction in the last ten years. More and more writers are thinking about the changes that will be brought about by nano-technology.

One common theme is a *programmable dust*, which when dropped on a pile of raw materials can reshape that pile of materi-als into roads, bridges, machines, or food. Remember, I said this was science fiction. But it turns out that Intel is funding research by professors at Carnegie-Mellon to create machines that can form themselves into any shape. You scan something in one location, send the digital scan to another, and a three-dimensional object forms. Right now, the "dust" is rather large egg-sized objects. It's still just in progress. But people at Intel feel they will be able to re-duce the size over time. They are talking in terms of ten to twenty years. These are serious people and serious money looking at pro-jects that seem to be right out of *Star Wars*.

I do recognize that there is another side of science fiction (mostly of the cyberpunk subgenre)—the dark side of the biotech and nanotech developments. It will be increasingly easy for some-one to do something that will be profoundly destructive. Preventing these types of problems, and mere accidents, will be one of the more profound challenges of the next thirty years.

Dovetailing with the Biotech Revolution is the drive for new en-ergy sources. $100 oil is not the problem; it's the solution, as con-verting to new energy sources is a huge growth dynamic. The need for new and cheaper sources of energy will compel all sorts of in-novation and new invention. The steam engine was basically devel-oped to pump water out of coalmines, because England needed new forms of energy to substitute for dwindling forests. Yet the collateral uses propelled the British Empire to its peak of economic power. Think of the resources and the money and the innovations that will come to play with the development of a new energy paradigm for the world.

There is a consortium that is starting work on a nuclear fusion power plant in France. This is a huge, $10 billion-plus project. They are working on a twenty-year timeline. But fusion will provide an almost unlimited amount of clean, environmentally friendly, and cheap power. But I deeply suspect that in the meantime smaller, less well-funded inventors will surprise us.

An article in *The Scotsman* reports, "A team of scientists has discovered a completely new way to make electricity from nothing more than flowing water. The breakthrough, the first new method of electricity production for 160 years, could provide free, clean energy for devices such as mobile phones and calculators. On a large scale, it could conceivably be used to feed power into the national grid. Dr David Lynch, Dean of the Faculty of Engineering at the University of Alberta in Canada, where the technology was developed, said: 'The discovery of an entirely new way of producing power is an incredible fundamental research breakthrough that occurs once in a lifetime. . . . The system relies on the natural "electrokinetic" effect of a fluid flowing over a solid surface. An interplay of forces results in a thin layer of water—where it meets the surface—with a net electric charge.' "[8]

For the first time in history, we could get multiple major Innovation Booms—the Information, Biotech, Quantum, and Energy Waves—all creating change and economic progress at the same time. It would be like Watts and Edison and Ford and Bell and Whitney and Crick all doing their thing at the same time. How different might our world have been? How would things have progressed? Just imagining the possibilities will give you some idea of what may lie in our future.

Not all of the waves of change will be technological. A great deal of the Millennium Wave, and perhaps the more profoundly disruptive, will be the changes in society. These will be brought about because of the inevitable consequences of demographics, and the increase in globalization combined with significant geopolitical changes.

DEMOGRAPHY IS DESTINY

Another thing that is cooked into the books is demography. We can make a fairly realistic projection of how many people will be over 60 in twenty years by looking at how many people are over 40 today. By projecting birth and death rates, which change slowly over time, we can get a fairly realistic handle on world population trends. And what we see is an aging Europe, Japan, and America, and a slowdown in the birth rates almost everywhere.

This will have a major effect on the pace and shift of globalization. The developed countries (North America, Europe, and Japan) have gone from about 33 percent of world population in 1950 to the 18 percent range right now. The current developed countries will be 12 percent of the population in forty-five years. The current underdeveloped countries (many well on the way to being fully developed) are going to grow to roughly 87 percent. That's a huge shift of economic power and markets.

Another important shift will be in the ten major Islamic countries. By 2050 their population will be about the same as the developed countries. Today, Russia has 145 million people; at its current rate, it will be 100 million in 2050. Iran and Iraq currently have 87 million people combined. Today they are roughly 60 percent of the population of Russia, and in just 2025 those two countries will have 10 million more people than Russia. Iran alone will have a greater population than Russia in forty-five years. How do you think a nuclear and militaristic power like Russia is going to be able to deal with that change? It makes me wonder if the reason Iran wants nuclear power is simply the United States.

Yemen is projected to have a population bigger than Germany in forty-five years. Yemen is a small country; where will the people go?[8] It is almost physically impossible for Yemen to grow from 18,000,000 to a UN-projected 84,000,000 people. Either birth rates must slow down dramatically, or they will have to migrate. This problem will be duplicated many times over.

We have already witnessed the largest migration of humanity in human history. More than 200 million Chinese have moved from the interior and the west to within 90 miles of the coast in the last

20 years. That is almost too large to grasp. It is as if almost all of the population of the middle part of United States decided to move to the coast. The clear implication of demographic change is that we will see more migration of people. Part of this will be caused by the need of developing countries, whose populations are aging, for workers.

What implications does demography have on the aging population of the world? The percentage of population over 60 years old will grow dramatically in the developed world from 2005 to 2040. The United States will go from 16 percent today over the age of 60 to 26 percent; Japan grows from 23 percent to 44 percent; Italy grows from 24 percent to 46 percent. Given that some of the population will be below age 20 and/or in school, that is less than one worker per retired person in many European countries. Besides the problem of who will pay for retirement benefits, there is the problem of who will be available to take care of the elderly. There simply will not be enough workers without massive immigration in many countries.

The Center for Strategic and International Studies notes that "for most of human history, until about a century ago, the elderly (people aged 65 and over) never amounted to more than 2 or 3 percent of the population."[9]

These are major problems that will affect worker productivity, affect health care, and strain the economy. The percentage of GDP that countries will have to tax if they keep the promises they made to the retirees will be a problem, as there will be less workers to pay into the pay-as-you-go retirement systems. France will be at 64 percent and Germany will be at 60 percent of GDP just for social services, without adding other government costs such as education, military, roads, and so on.

Bluntly, these countries (including the United States) simply will not be able to meet their current commitments. That means either significant tax increases or large benefit cuts or a combination of both.

Do you think young, educated entrepreneurial people are going to stay in France or Germany and see tax rates of 75 percent or more? The strain on the systems clearly can't work.[10] Europe and

Japan are destined to go through enormous social and economic strains. Farm subsidies, a deeply engrained part of Europe and Japan, will be cut or done away with. How can I say this? There will be more elderly voters who want their health care and pensions than there are farmers. Just the threat of a drop of a small part of farm subsidies in France brings out farmers who riot, block roads, and create mass protests. Think about what will happen as they lose those subsidies over the next ten to fifteen years.

Although not as bad as Europe and Japan, the United States has its own problems coming down the demographic highway. The United States will be forced to change its Social Security system. If we don't change it by the end of 2006, my prediction is that it will not change until 2013. Whoever is elected president by either party in 2008 will not touch the "third rail" of politics (Social Security) until a second term. By then, the problems will be much bigger.

Social Security in the United States can be fixed. The real problem is Medicare and health care. Health care costs will rise from 14 percent of GDP in 2003 to 17 percent in 2010 and keep on rising as Baby Boomers need more care and as better and ever more expensive solutions are found to keep us healthy. This portends a massive shift in consumer spending patterns.

A reported $40 trillion deficit to pay for Medicare looms in front of U.S. taxpayers. The options are not pretty. We can raise taxes significantly over time, cut back on other spending like our military, farm subsidies, education and welfare, or cut back on health care. What politician will want to run on that platform?

And there are even more profound cultural changes, as documented in a book I highly recommend called *Fewer* by Ben Wattenberg. The book is based on the implications of a new UN projection of future population growth. Prior to 2002, the United Nations assumed that worldwide population growth would slow to about 2.1 children per woman. Now it is assumed that worldwide population growth will be 1.85. (2.1 is the replacement level, by the way.) That number is the *total fertility rate*, or TFR.

The TFR of what the United States considers the more developed countries (basically the countries thought of as the West and Japan) is 1.6, well below replacement rate. The United States has the highest rate among all these countries at 2.0, while Europe as a whole is only 1.38. Using a slightly higher TFR for Europe, or 1.45, European population is expected decline from 728 million people today to about 632 million by 2050.

But this trend is not limited to developed countries: The rest of the world is moving to lower fertility rates at a very rapid pace. While most everyone is aware that China has had its TFR drop to around 1.8 because of the one-child policy, I was surprised to read that Iran has dropped from a TFR of 7.0 in 1960 to just 2.1 today! Egypt has watched its TFR drop in half in the last forty years, to slightly above 3.0, and it is dropping every year. Brazil is now below the replacement level of 2.1. India has seen its TFR dropped from 6.0 to just over 3.0 in only a few decades and the trend is decidedly down, especially among the new Indian middle-class.

Demographers in Mexico expect the TFR of our southern neighbor to drop below replacement level this year! Think about what that means for U.S. immigration policy in twenty years. South Korea has gone from a TFR of 6.3 in the late 1950s to only 1.17 in 2003. Russia is at 1.1. Bulgaria is at 1.1. Japan is at 1.3. Germany is at 1.35. All told, there are sixty-three nations whose TFR is below 2.1.

I suppose it intellectually follows that a low birth rate will mean that there will be a high percentage of women who have no children. I was rather surprised, though, by the number of women with no children at the end of their childbearing years: Germany 26 percent, Finland 21 percent, United Kingdom 21 percent, Italy 19 percent, Netherlands 19 percent, and Canada 14 percent. The United States stands at 16 percent, up from 11 percent in the early 1970s.

There is a stark contrast between retirement in Europe and retirement in the United States. Today, retirement age is traditionally 65 in the United States. The retirement age (for Social Security benefits) was raised in the United States in 1983 to 67, which will take full effect by 2022. The following are examples of the average retirement age for men in Europe: Belgium, 58.1; France, 58.8; Germany 61.0; Italy and the Netherlands are slightly under 60; United Kingdom, 62.9; in Switzerland, 64.5.

Wattenberg makes the point that a nation whose population is not growing and is not increasing its tax base and economic base cannot continue to thrive. The United States needs its immigrants. Without them, our Social Security and Medicare problems are greatly increased to the severe breaking point. We could see our problems become as large as Europe's. Forgetting the cultural implications, and from a pure economic standpoint, the United States should be aggressively seeking to increase immigration of the right kind. Our policy today is haphazard and ill informed, but at least allows for one million immigrants per year. If we were smart, we would be doing everything we could to get young, educated people to come to the United States, as well as educating our own children better.

It is a far different world in Europe. Quoting from Wattenberg: ". . . consider Europe, according to [a UN publication called] 'Replacement Migration.' Today, Europe has more than twice as many people as the United States, but the whole continent takes in a net of 376,000 immigrants per year, about a third of the American number. In order to keep a total constant population, that European immigration number would have to rise to 1,917,000 per year, an annual increase of more than 500 percent. To maintain a constant age group of workers aged 15 to 64, the number of immigrants would have to rise to 3,227,000 per year, an annual increase of more than 900 percent. The United Nations also calculated what it would take to keep the dependency ratio constant—that is, the proportions of working-age persons to those over age 65 and under 15. That would require an annual immigration of 27,139,000, an increase of more than 7100 percent. That is not likely to happen."[11]

Quite the understatement. Forget about energy. We will one day see that young people are the true natural and limited resource.

Demographics cannot be legislated against. Demonstrations will not change their reality. These trends are going to force profound changes on our countries and cultures, as well as our economies.

As an aside, culturally the new demographics means there will be big changes in the way we look at family and marriage. On a variety of levels, this is going to be difficult, as it will be seen as an assault on traditional marriage. But if we are talking about *traditional* as in the historical model, and still the model in many places in the world today, where the woman is more or less property and has no rights, then a little redefinition of traditional is needed. As Stephanie Coontz points out in *Marriage: A History*, it has only been relatively recently (in terms of human history) that we see people marrying for love. Already, we are seeing a significant difference in marriage rates, as women put off marrying longer and longer, as well as forgo having children. The independence of women (a very good thing!) has produced a new dynamic in relationships that has yet to settle out. These are changes with unintended consequences that we will only learn about as we see them unfold.

THE GLOBALIZATION WAVE

Globalization refers to the increasing economic integration and interdependence of countries. Economic globalization in this century has proceeded along two main lines: trade liberalization (the increased circulation of goods) and financial liberalization (the expanded circulation of capital).

We are familiar with the problem of U.S. manufacturing jobs going to China, as well as service jobs being outsourced to India. Each factory that closes down has the local news team at its door when the announcement is made.

But what we do not focus on is the fact that more jobs are outsourced *to* the United States from foreign countries than the other way around. Globalization has many aspects, but it means that everything is going to change even faster. Tom Friedman has it right in his best-selling book, *The World Is Flat*. He notes that new technologies have enabled new processes that make it easier to do business anywhere in the world. The playing field for business has become horizontal:

> Just as we finished creating this new, more horizontal playing field, and companies and individuals primarily in the West started quickly adapting to it, 3 billion people who had been frozen out of the field suddenly found themselves liberated to plug-and-play with everybody else.

Save for a tiny minority, these 3 billion people had never been allowed to compete and collaborate before, because they lived in largely closed economies with very vertical, hierarchical political and economic structures. I'm talking about the people of China, India, Russia, Eastern Europe, Latin America, and Central Asia. Their economies and political systems all opened up during the course of the 1990s, so that their people were increasingly free to join the free market game. And when did these 3 billion people converge with the new playing field in the new processes? Right when the field was being flattened, right when millions of them could compete and collaborate more equally, more horizontally, and with cheaper and more readily available tools than ever before. Indeed, thanks to the flattening of the world, many of these new entrants didn't even have to leave home to participate . . . the playing field came to them!

It is this triple convergence—of new players, on a new playing field, developing new processes and habits for horizontal collaboration—that I believe is the most important force shaping global economies and politics in the early 21st century. Giving so many people access to all these tools of collaboration, along with the ability through search engines and the Web to access billions of pages of raw information, ensures that the next generation of innovations will come from all over Planet Flat. The scale of the global community that is soon going to be able to participate in all sorts of discovery and innovation is something the world has simply never seen before.[12]

The pace of globalization is going to change. Apart from governments interfering with protectionist legislation, there is little to stop the trend. But this has produced some severe imbalances in the world. Right now, the United States is running a huge trade deficit, absorbing the products and the savings of the developing world. This is a trend that simply cannot go on forever. The shift from a U.S.-centric world to a more balanced world is going to create a great deal of pain and opportunity, but when the world does sort it out (and it will, if not easily!) we will have a more balanced world economy.

This will all produce a shift of economic power to the East. China, India, and the rest of Asia will come to the fore by the middle of this century. This shift will be forced because of the economic, political, and demographic changes that will happen in the West. The United States and Europe have guaranteed our Baby Boomers and our elders "X" amount of our GDP. We have bet the farm on our future, yet we haven't saved enough money for it and we're expecting our kids to pay it. That's going to force fundamental restructuring. China, India, and other parts of Asia don't have those obligations because the elderly population is a much smaller percentage, so they will be able to devote more of their dollars to research and to economic development. It will be many years before their R&D budgets equal those in the West, but over time, the advantage the West has will be reduced.

A NEW WORLD ORDER

James Dale Davidson and Lord William Rees-Mogg wrote these very prescient words in *The Sovereign Individual* in 1997:

> In short, the future is likely to confound the expectations of those who have absorbed the civic myths of 20th-century industrial society. Among them are the illusions of social democracy that once thrilled and motivated the most gifted minds. They presuppose that societies evolve in whatever way governments wished them to—preferably in response to opinion polls of scrupulously counted votes. This was never as true as it seemed 50 years ago. Now it is an anachronism, as much an artifact of industrialism as a rusting smokestack. The civic myths reflect not only a mindset that sees society's problems as susceptible to engineering solutions; they also reflect a false confidence that resources and individuals will remain as vulnerable to political compulsion in the future as they have been in the 20th century. We doubt it. *Market forces, not political majorities, will compel societies to reconfigure themselves in ways that public opinion will neither comprehend nor welcome.*[13]

The waves of new technologies, demographics, and globalization are going to force a wave of government changes that as Davidson and Rees-Mogg state: *". . . will compel societies to reconfigure themselves in ways that public opinion will neither comprehend nor welcome."*

Governments are the problem, not the solution. If government is the answer, then we are asking the wrong question. Less government, from a business standpoint, generally means less cost, and that is a better thing. The less money that you are paying in taxes, the less money your corporations and your investors pay in taxes, the more the customers are going to be able to pay to put your products on the table and in their homes. Not to mention the more money to return to investors. And that means more opportunity for everyone.

We are going to have to learn to reallocate resources. That means that some people will not be getting the government aid they thought they had been promised. That is a change few will like. But there will be no choice. At some point, reality will meet with expectations. Reality always wins.

"The economic and financial world is changing in ways that we still do not fully comprehend," Greenspan told a recent bankers' conference in Beijing. "Policymakers accordingly cannot always count on an ability to anticipate potentially adverse developments sufficiently in advance to effectively address them."[14]

How do you deal with the Millennium Wave and the changes it will bring? First, recognize that change is an opportunity. It will create new prospects for work, investment, and your life. But it will also require you to understand that sometimes change is going to be thrust upon you. This process has already started and is only going to increase in size.

Some economists have been slow to recognize the new order of employment, but it hasn't escaped everyone. Erica Groshen and Simon Potter of the New York Fed summarized the situation in August 2003: "We find evidence of structural change in two features of the 2001 recession: the predominance of permanent job losses over temporary layoffs and the relocation of jobs from one industry to another" (which is a far different pattern than previous recessions). The data suggest that most of the jobs added in the recovery have been new positions in different firms and industries, not rehires.

Instead of "layoff, then rehire," the economy must: "fire, retrain (if possible), move, and hire." They write: "An unusually high share of unemployed workers must now find new positions in different firms or industries. The task of finding such jobs, difficult and time-consuming under the best of conditions, is likely to be even more complicated now, when financial market weakness and economic uncertainty prevail."[15]

Therefore, you must realize that change requires flexibility. The Millennium Wave will require constant learning and relearning. College is now just the beginning of an education. Very few people will have a job that will not change substantially over time. And that is a good thing, because if you keep up with the changing world, it will create opportunity.

I keep using that word—opportunity. But that is the right way to look at the Millennium Wave. It would be all too easy to focus on the negative aspects of the changes that are coming our way, and there are a lot of them. But focusing on the negative will not work in the coming years. In fact, it has not been a good strategy in the past.

WHAT THIS MEANS FOR INVESTORS

Albert Wang in an article in the 2001 Academy of Sciences *Journal of Financial Intermediation* shows us that a cautious optimism is the appropriate approach. Wang uses evolutionary game theory to study the population dynamics of a securities market. In his model, the growth rate of wealth accumulation drives the evolutionary process, and is endogenously determined (by that it means that only the data and not some outside factors influenced the determination of winners and losers). He finds that neither underconfident investors nor bearish sentiment can survive in the market. Massively overconfident or bullish investors are also incapable of long-run survival. However, investors who are only moderately overconfident can actually come to dominate the market!

In the world of our ancestors, overconfidence would get you killed. Lack of confidence would mean you sat around and starved. Cautious optimism was the right approach!

And it still is.

The Millennium Wave is also going to offer the greatest investment opportunities ever seen, as whole new companies and processes are created. Of course, this means that what Schumpeter called "creative destruction" will be in full force, as many companies become the buggy whip manufacturers of the new century. Taking advantage of all these changes will require a nimbleness and an ability to make decisions, rather than passively investing in indexes, which will reflect the companies that have already become large or are getting ready to go the way of dinosaurs.

Change. You'd better get to know and love it. It is coming. That is one thing that for certain will not change.

NOTES

Chapter 3

1. Two important papers confirm the importance of style: one by William F. Sharpe analyzing 395 mutual funds and one by Roger Ibbotson analyzing 3,100 funds. Both studies confirmed that style could explain 90 percent of the variation in returns. The specific stocks chosen by the manager explained only 10 percent of the monthly variation in return.

2. Technically, the information ratio it is the ratio of the average excess return over an appropriate benchmark to the variability of that average excess return. The importance of the information ratio as a theoretical construct has been developed at length over a very long time starting in the early 1970s (see Treynor-Black, 1973; Brealey & Hodges, 1973; Ambechtscheer, 1974; Ferguson, 1975; and Rosenberg, 1976.)

3. The interpretation of the information ratio is conceptually related to a t-statistic. The t-statistic is a term (scalar) for the difference between a random variable and its mean, divided by the standard deviation of the random variable. When the random variable is estimated from a population of n observations and the standard deviation is estimated from the residual variability of that population, the resulting ratio has a well-known distribution called the t-distribution. Consequently, the t-statistic can be used to do a test of whether the random variable differs significantly from the hypothesized mean. Where the number of observations, n, is greater than 30, the distribution is quite close to the normal distribution. When using a t-statistic for skill or information content, we are looking for large positive values of the statistic that urge us to reject the null hypothesis that no skill or information is present (that the mean is zero).

4. See William F. Sharpe, "Capital Asset Prices: A Theory of Market Equilibrium under Conditions of Risk," *Journal of Finance* 19 (1964), 425–442.

5. In order to understand how to use the information ratio, we must discuss the effect of time. Suppose that a manager can outperform the market (or, more precisely, a passive benchmark appropriate to the manager's strategy) by 2 percent per year. This is an "alpha of 2 percent." Suppose also that the manager takes a certain level of active risk to achieve this. In other words, the standard deviation of the difference between the manager's annual performance and the performance of a benchmark—which is called the tracking error—is 6 percent. This is a realistic value for active managers who have a chance of producing an alpha of 2 percent, but who manage diversified portfolios. Then in a typical year, the ratio (alpha/tracking error) is one-third. This ratio is a measure of pure skill. How long will it take, with this amount of skill, for a manager's performance history to have an expected t-statistic of 2.0, which is a common measure of statistical significance? This requires that the ratio be 2.0. For a cumulative performance history over a number of years, the alpha is not affected. However, the standard deviation around that alpha is reduced by the square root of the number of years. In order to increase the ratio from 1/3 to 2, or by a factor of six, 36 years is required. In order to gain an expected t-statistic of 2.5, or the 99 percent confidence level, the one-year ratio must be increased by a factor of 7.5. To accomplish this, 56 years is required. For more information, see Chapter 5.

6. See Ronald Kahn and Andrew Rudd, "Does Historical Performance Predict Future Performance?" *Financial Analysts Journal* (November/December, 1995), 43–52.

7. This calculation is available upon request at jfinn@vantage consultinggroup.com.

Chapter 6

1. Largely thanks to the work of Joseph LeDoux; see his wonderful book for details. *The Emotional Brain: The Mysterious Underpinnings of Emotional Life* (New York: Simon & Schuster, 1998).

2. For more on this, see Paul Ekman, *Emotions Revealed: Recognizing Faces and Feelings to Improve Communication and Emotional Life* (New York: Owl Books, 2004).

It is also worth noting that some developmental psychologists have designed programs to teach children to recognize the physical signs of emotions (such as anger) and then use thought to control those emotions. See Mark Greenberg's work at Pennsylvania State University, Harrisburg Center for Healthy Child Development Prevention Research Center, "PATHS Curriculum" (www.prevention.psu.edu/projects/PATHScurriculum.htm). Much of the work has focused on teaching children to constrain their anger—a modern-day equivalent of counting to ten.

3. N. Epley and T. Gilovich, "Putting Adjustment Back in the Anchoring and Adjustment Heuristic," *Psychological Science*, vol. 12, no. 5 (2001), 391–396.

4. D. T. Gilbert and M. J. Gill, "The Momentary Realist," *Psychological Science*, vol. 11, no. 5 (2000), 394–398.

5. For more on this, see Antonio R. Damasio, *Descartes' Error: Emotion, Reason, and the Human Brain* (New York: Quill, 1995).

6. A. Bechara, H. Damasio, D. Tranel, and A. R. Damasio, "Deciding Advantageously before Knowing the Advantageous Strategy," *Science*, 275 (1997).

7. Antoine Bechara, Hanna Damasio, Antonio R. Damasio, George Loewenstein, and Baba Shiv, "Investment Behavior and the Dark Side of Emotion," unpublished paper (2004).

8. Technically speaking, this group had suffered lesions to the amygdala, orbitofrontal, and insular/somatosensory cortex—all parts of the X-system.

9. Colin Camerer, George Loewenstein, and Drazen Prelec, "Neuroeconomics: How Neuroscience Can Inform Economics," *Journal of Economic Literature*, Vol. XLIII (March 2005), 9–64.

10. G. Loewenstein, D. Nagin, and R. Paternoster, "The Effect of Sexual Arousal on Expectations of Sexual Forcefulness," *Journal of Research in Crime and Delinquency*, vol. 34, no. 4 (1997).

11. M. Muraven and R. F. Baumeister, "Self-Regulation and Depletion of Limited Resources: Does Self-Control Resemble a Muscle?" *Psychological Bulletin*, vol. 126, no. 2 (2000). Also, R. F. Baumeister, "The Psychology of Irrationality: Why People Make Foolish, Self-Defeating Choices," in Isabelle Brocas and Juan D. Carrillo, *The Psychology of Economic Decision Volume I: Rationality and Well-Being* (Oxford University Press: 2003).

12. Baumeister (2003).
13. R. F. Baumeister, E. Bratslavsky, M. Muraven, and D. M. Tice. "Ego Depletion: Is the Active Self a Limited Resource?" *Journal of Personality and Social Psychology*, vol. 74 (1998), 1252–1265. Reprinted with permission.
14. E. Pronin, D. Y. Lin, L. Ross, "The Bias Blind Spot: Perceptions of Bias in Self versus Others," *Personality and Social Psychology Bulletin*, vol. 28 (2002).
15. D. Hirschleifer, "Investor Psychology and Asset Pricing," *Journal of Finance*, vol. 56 (2001).
16. Paul Slovic, "Behavioral Problems of Adhering to Decision Policy," unpublished manuscript (1973).
17. Gustaf Torngren and Henry Montgomery, "Worse than Chance? Performance and Confidence among Professionals and Laypeople in the Stock Market," *Journal of Behavioural Finance*, vol. 5 (2004).
18. A. Tversky and D. Griffin, "The Weighing of Evidence and the Determinants of Confidence," *Cognitive Psychology*, vol. 24 (1992), 411–435.
19. A. Tversky and D. Kahneman, "Judgment under Uncertainty, Heuristics and Biases," *Science*, vol. 185 (1974).
20. G. Northcraft and M. A. Neale, "Experts, Amateurs, and Real Estate," *Organizational Behaviour and Human Decisions Processes*, vol. 39 (1987).
21. Dan Ariely, George F. Loewenstein, and Drazen Prelec, "Coherent Arbitrariness: Stable Demand Curves without Stable Preferences," *Quarterly Journal of Economics*, vol. 118 (2003).
22. It draws on work by L. Chan, J. Karceski, and J. Lakonishok, "The Level and Persistence of Growth Rates," *Journal of Finance*, vol. 58 (2003), 634–684.
23. Louis K. C. Chan, Jason J. Karceski, and Josef Lakonishok, "The Level and Persistence of Growth Rates," *Journal of Finance*, vol. 58 (2003), 643–684.
24. Uri Simonsohn, Niklas Karlsson, George F. Loewenstein, and Dan Ariely, "The Tree of Experience in the Forest of Information," available from www.ssrn.com (2004).
25. For more on this see the work of Daniel Simons, the leader in this field: http://viscog.beckman.uiuc.edu/djs_lab/.

26. Daniel J. Simons and Christopher F. Chabris, "Gorillas in Our Midst: Sustained Inattentional Blindness for Dynamic Events," *Perception*, vol. 28 (1999).

27. D. Kahneman, J. Knetsch, and R. Thaler, "Experimental Tests of the Endowment Effect and the Coase Theorem," *Journal of Political Economy*, vol. 98 (1990).

28. Ibid., and Robert Franciosi, Praveen Kujal, Roland Michelitsch, Vernon Smith, and Gang Deng, "Experimental Tests of the Endowment Effect," *Journal of Economic Behaviour and Organization*, vol. 30 (1996).

29. Prospect theory is the most frequently used behavioral alternative to classical economics. It incorporates loss aversion neatly.

30. Hersh Shefrin and Meir Statman, "The Disposition to Sell Winners Too Early and Ride Losers Too Long: Theory and Evidence," *Journal of Finance*, vol. 40 (1985).

31. Terrance Odean, "Are Investors Reluctant to Realize Their Losses," *Journal of Finance* (October 1998).

32. Terrance Odean, Brad M. Barber, and Ju Zheng, "The Behavior of Mutual Fund Investors," unpublished paper (2001).

33. Andrea Frazzini, "The Disposition Effect and Underreaction to News," *Journal of Finance*, Yale IFC working paper, available from www.ssrn.com (2004).

Chapter 8

1. CAPM is an economic theory that describes the relationship between risk and expected return, and serves as a model for the pricing of risky securities. The CAPM asserts that the only risk that is priced by rational investors is systematic risk, because that risk cannot be eliminated by diversification. The CAPM says that the expected return of a security or a portfolio is equal to the rate on a risk-free security plus a risk premium multiplied by the asset's systematic risk. The theory was invented by William Sharpe (1964) and John Lintner (1965). The early work of Jack Treynor was also instrumental in the development of this model.

2. Group 1 drops from a valuation of $100 to $67. Group 2 increases from a valuation of $100 to $200. Total profit is $67 on a total $200 portfolio, or 33%.

Chapter 12

1. Dr. Alan Krueger, "Economic Scene: Rapid Productivity Growth Probably Did Not Cause Slow Post-Recession Job Growth." *New York Times* (November 13, 2003), Section C, p. 2.
2. http://www.kurzweilai.net/articles/art0134.html?printable=1.
3. *Wall Street Journal* (June 29, 2005), page 1.
4. Michael A. Alexander, *Stock Cycles: Why Stocks Won't Beat Money Markets over the Next Twenty Years* (Lincoln, NE: iUniverse.com, 2000).
5. Harry S. Dent Jr., *The Roaring 2000s: Building the Wealth and Lifestyle You Desire in the Greatest Boom in History* (New York: Simon & Schuster, 1998).
6. Study done by Crestmont Research, www.crestmontresearch.com.
7. Dalbar Inc., www.dalbar.com.
8. John Innes, "Scientists Find Way to Power Mobile Phones by Water," *The Scotsman* (October 20, 2003). http://news.scotsman.com/archive.cfm?id=1158372003.
9. Martin Barnes, *The Bank Credit Analyst* (March 2003), www.bcaresearch.com.
10. Richard Jackson and Neil Howe, "The 2003 Aging Vulnerability Index: An Assessment of the Capacity of Twelve Developed Countries to Meet the Aging Challenge," Center for Strategic and International Studies (CSIS) (March 2003).
11. Ben J. Fewer and Ivan R. Wattenberg, *Fewer: How the New Demography of Depopulation Will Shape Our Future* (December 2004), 37.
12. Thomas L. Friedman, *The World Is Flat* (New York: Farrar, Strauss and Giroux, 2005), 181.
13. James Dale Davidson and Lord William Rees-Mogg, *The Sovereign Individual* (New York: Simon & Schuster, 1997), 25–26.
14. Greenspan speaking before an International Monetary Conference in Beijing, China, June 2005, and also available at www.federalreserve.gov.
15. http://www.newyorkfed.org/research/current_issues/ci9-8.pdf.

INDEX